studying the
BIBLE

Karyn Henley

Studying the
BIBLE   **The foundation**
for knowing God

Written by Karyn Henley
Cover design by Brian Fowler
Illustrations by Jeff Richardson
Cover and inside illustrations by Ed Koehler

The dandelion logo is a trademark of Karyn Henley.

For more information about this curriculum, contact: office@karynhenley.com

www.KarynHenley.com

ISBN 978-1-933803-20-3

TABLE OF CONTENTS

	Introduction	5
	Suggested Bible Study Helps	8
1	Where Did the Bible Come From?	9
	Romans 15:4	
2	Versions and Paraphrases	15
	2 Timothy 3:16	
3	Book by Book, Part 1	21
	John 21:25	
4	Book by Book, Part 2	27
	Isaiah 40:8	
5	Seeking God and His Ways, Part 1	32
	Jeremiah 29: 13	
6	Seeking God and His Ways, Part 2	39
	James 4:8	
7	Study by Topics	45
	Deuteronomy 32:46, 47	
8	Character Study	51
	1 John 1:1	
9	Places and Times	56
	Mark 13:31	
10	Synoptic and Chronological Bibles	71
	Psalm 19:7, 8, 10	
11	The Bible in My Life	78
	Psalm 119: 105	
12	Guided Devotions	85
	John 20:31	
13	Making Plans	90
	Matthew 4:4	

INTRODUCTION

The Irish poet William Butler Yeats once said, "Education is not the filling of a pail, but the lighting of a fire." In the first temple, the tent of meeting, there was a lampstand. God's instructions were, "Tell the people of Israel to bring you pure olive oil for the lampstand, so it can be kept burning continually…Aaron and his sons will keep the lamps burning in the Lord's presence day and night" (Exodus 27:20, 21, NLT). Today we are God's temple (1 Corinthians 3:16). And our passion, our living love for the Lord, keeps our lampstand burning before him. (See Revelation 2:4, 5.) Our job in the spiritual education of children is to light a fire, a living, growing love for God within them.

The Foundations curriculum can help light that fire. Each of our children is a temple of God. So the goal of the Foundations curriculum is to construct within children the essential foundations upon which they can build (and sustain) a loving, thriving relationship with the Lord. To do this, the Foundations curriculum provides a thorough, step-by-step, in-depth exploration of the following foundations:

Studying the Bible, The Foundation for Knowing God
Prayer, The Foundation for Growing Closer to God
Worship, The Foundation for Loving God
Lordship, The Foundation for Following God
Missions, The Foundation for Sharing God
Stewardship, The Foundation for Reflecting God
Making Peace, The Foundation for Living in Fellowship

This curriculum is intended for use with students in third through fifth grades. Each quarter is independent of the others, so they can be taught in any order. In fact, each quarter can be used as a single unit to fill in a 13-week study at any time of the year and can be followed or preceded by any other curriculum of your choice.

To round out a 2-year sequence we suggest using *The Compass*, a 13-week study for the same age group covering the love of God as expressed through Jesus.

WALK THROUGH A WEEK

SCRIPTURE AND GOAL

The session begins with a Scripture and a simple goal. You may use the Scripture as a memory verse if you wish, or you may use it to support the theme for the day, reading the Scripture when you gather for the first prayer.

INTRODUCTORY ACTIVITY

You can begin your introductory activity as soon as the first student arrives, guiding others to join you as they come into your room. This activity serves two purposes. First it gives children something fun to do from the first moment they arrive. Second, it starts thoughts and conversations about the theme of the session. Talking is encouraged. Questions are welcome. Get to know your students. Make it your goal to discover something interesting and special about each one. Let them know that their mission is to discover more about God and about how they can get to know Him better every day, so that God becomes their constant companion, their treasured friend, their awesome King.

DISCOVERY RALLY

Gather the children together as a group now in preparation for the Discovery Centers.

What's the Good Word? This is a time to read the Scripture for the day. You may also sing a few songs if you want.

Challenge. This is a time to introduce the children to the theme for the day by making challenging statements or asking challenging questions.

Prayer. Choose a student to lead a prayer of blessing for the day's activities, asking God to open your hearts and teach everyone present.

DISCOVERY CENTERS

You will need either one teacher/facilitator for each group, or clearly written instructions that tell the children what they are to do in the group.

The way your class uses discovery centers will depend on how much time you have and how many children there are in your class.

- If you have a few students, go together to as many centers as you can in the time you have.
- If you have more than ten students and lots of time, divide into three groups. Send one group to each center and let each group rotate to a different center as they finish the activity, so that each student gets to go to each center during Discovery Center time.
- If you have more than ten students, but little time, divide into groups of three. Number off, one to three in each group. Each student #1 goes to the first center, #2 goes to the second, #3 goes to the third. After each center has completed its activity, the original groups of three come back together again to tell each other what they learned in their centers.
- Or you may choose to let all three centers do the same activity. Choose the one or two activities that you think your students will enjoy most. Divide the students into groups for centers, and once they are there, do not rotate. Instead, let each group do the one or two activities you have chosen.

DEBRIEFING QUESTIONS

If you have time, gather together as a large group at the end of the class time to ask and answer questions and discuss the theme and/or other issues on the children's minds.

Review the Scripture for the day.

PRAY

You or a student may close your class time in prayer.

SUGGESTED BIBLE STUDY HELPS

This is by no means a complete list. As you look for these, you will find others that may be just as interesting and helpful.

Bible Handbooks

What the Bible is All About, Henrietta Mears (Gospel Light)
What the Bible is All About for Young Explorers, Frances Blankenbaker (Gospel Light)
The International Children's Bible Handbook, Lawrence O. Richards (Word)
The Baker Bible Handbook for Kids (Baker)
New Unger's Bible Handbook: Student Edition, Merrill Unger (Moody)

Bible Encyclopedias

The Children's Bible Encyclopedia: The Bible Made Simple and Fun, Mark Water (Baker Books)

Bible Dictionaries

International Children's Bible Dictionary, Lynn Waller (Word)
The Baker Bible Dictionary for Kids (Baker)

Bible Fact Books

The Awesome Book of Bible Facts, Sandy Silverthorne (Harvest House)
The Baker Book of Bible People (Baker)
The Complete Book of Bible Trivia, J. Stephen Lang (Tyndale)

For Teachers and Older Students

Willmington's Bible Handbook, Harold L. Willmington (Tyndale)
Holman's Topical Concordance (Holman Bible Publishers)
Holman Bible Dictionary (Holman Bible Publishers)
Children's Ministry Resource Edition (Thomas Nelson)
Manners and Customs in the Bible, Victor H. Matthews (Hendrickson)

Where Did the Bible Come From?

Scripture

"Everything that was written in the past was written to teach us, so that we could have hope." Romans 15:4, ICB

Goal

Learn that the Bible was written with a variety of tools on a variety of surfaces, and it was written over a long period of time.

INTRODUCTION

As the students arrive, give each one a piece of paper. Have markers and crayons available. Ask each one to write the name of his favorite book's title in rebus form on the paper. A rebus is a sentence or story, or in this case a title, in which any words are represented in pictures where possible. For example, for *Little House on the Prairie*, the word *little* might be represented by a drawing of a ruler with a small number highlighted, the word *house* would be represented by a drawing of a house, the words *on* and *the* would be written as usual, and the word *prairie* would be drawn as a picture of a prairie. As the students finish, have them show their drawings to other students who try to guess what the title of that favorite book is.

Gather students together in a large group.

WHAT'S THE GOOD WORD?
Choose a student to read the Scripture for the day.

THE CHALLENGE
Bring one or more "bestseller" books to display, or bring a newspaper's list of the current week's bestseller books.

Ask: **What is a bestseller?** Explain that there is one book that has been the number one bestselling book for years, even for centuries. It's available in over one thousand seven hundred languages.

Ask: **Who can guess what that book is?** Allow time for responses. Then tell the students that the answer is the Bible.

Ask: **How did we get the Bible? How was it written?** Tell the students that in their Discovery Groups today, they will learn more about the Bible.

PRAYER

DISCOVERY CENTERS

1. MAKE A SCROLL

DO: Give each student two unsharpened pencils and one piece of plain paper. Direct the students to cut the paper in half lengthwise and tape the short ends together to make a long narrow piece of paper.

MATERIALS
unsharpened pencils, plain paper, scissors, transparent tape, markers and pens

Ask them to write the Scripture for today on the paper. Then they should tape each short end of this paper to a pencil and roll the pencil on each end toward the center of the paper. As each pencil rolls toward the center, the paper rolls around the pencils. When the pencils meet at the center, they form a scroll.

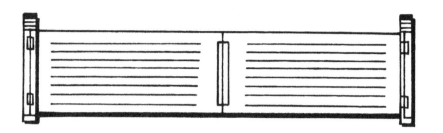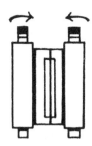

DISCUSS: As the students work, talk about the fact that the Bible was written over a period of about 1,500 years. The writers of the books of the Bible wrote on whatever the people of their times were writing on. Read or ask a student to read the following Scriptures to discover the kinds of materials used in the writing process.

- Ezekiel 4:1 (clay tablets)
- Exodus 24:12; Deuteronomy 27:2, 3; Joshua 8:32 (stone)
- 2 John 12 (papyrus)
- 2 Timothy 4:13 (animal skin, vellum/calfskin, parchment/lambskin, leather/cowhide
- Exodus 28:36; Job 19:24 (metal–gold, lead)

Explain that papyrus was made from two layers of papyrus reeds that had been split and pressed together to make a sheet.

Scrolls were made of papyrus, leather, or parchment. Read about scrolls in Exodus 17:14; Deuteronomy 17:18; 1 Samuel 10:25; Ezra 6:2; Job 19:23; Isaiah 8:1; Jeremiah 36; Ezekiel 2:9; Luke 4:17; and Revelation 1:11.

2. WRITING TOOLS

DO: Give each student a small paper plate, some clay, a few toothpicks, a feather, one piece of plain paper. Pour some paint into the small paper cups.

> **MATERIALS**
> small paper plates, clay, toothpicks, feathers, plain paper, water-based washable paint, bathroom-size paper cups

First, ask students to pat the clay out flat on the paper plate. Each student should write her name on a clay tablet using a toothpick as the writing tool, then write her name on paper using a feather as the writing tool. Students will dip the pointed quill end of the feather into the paint and write with the paint "ink."

DISCUSS: As the students are using these different writing tools, explain that in Bible times, most writing was done with a reed, straw, or feather with ink on papyrus or parchment, or with a stick-like stylus on clay or wax.

3. DATE THIS MANUSCRIPT

Before the session, copy each of the lines of Hebrew letters onto a different index card. On a separate copy or the Hebrew letters handout, add the following dates beside each line. This will be your master list.

MATERIALS
index cards, fine markers or pen, Hebrew Letters (page 14)

- Line 1: B.C. 1000
- Line 2: B.C. 925
- Line 3: B.C. 730
- Line 4: B.C. 600
- Line 5: B.C. 408
- Line 6: B.C. 275
- Line 7: A.D. 50
- Line 8: A.D. 130
- Line 9: A.D. 350
- Line 10: A.D.1895

These lines of letters show how some of the letters of the Hebrew alphabet have changed over the centuries.

Hide each of the cards in a different place in your classroom or outdoors.

DO: Tell the students to hunt for ancient manuscripts. Show them a card with the following letters and explain that they will be looking for similar cards.

When the students have found all the cards, they should compare the cards to the master list and try to date the "manuscripts" that they have found by finding which line it matches.

Then challenge them to do something a little more difficult. Say: **Look at the card I am holding and try to decide which lines my card should fit between. There are no lines that match it exactly.** (It fits between B.C. 275 and A.D. 50.) By looking closely, the students can see that the writing is similar to both of these. Kaf is similar to the B.C. 275. kaf, but lamed is more like the lamed of A.D. 50.

DISCUSS: Tell the students that this is exactly what people who find and study old writings do. Say: **The card I am holding contains letters taken from the Dead Sea Scrolls, the oldest copy of the book of Isaiah that has been found. The scholars, the ones who specialize in studying these writings, found how old the scrolls were by comparing the scroll's letters to letters from other writings whose age they already knew.** The students were comparing those same letters.

DISCOVERERS' DEBRIEFING:

If you have time to review, gather as a large group and discuss your young discoverers' findings. Ask the following questions:

- **What is the most interesting thing you discovered today?**
- **What is something you learned today that you didn't know before?**
- **Name some of the writing tools that people used in Bible times.**
- **Name some of the surfaces that ancient writers wrote on.**
- **When explorers discover an ancient writing (manuscript), how do they decide when it was written?**
- **Why is it important for researchers to know when a manuscript of the Bible was written?**

Review the Scripture for today.

Pray, thanking God for the discoveries of ancient manuscripts of the Bible, and for preserving his Word for us through the centuries.

IMPORTANT: Ask students to bring empty boxes (the size of cereal boxes–not snack size–rice boxes, instant potato boxes) next week. You will need 66 of these boxes for Session 3. It may help to send a note home with the students asking for these kinds of boxes.

Hebrew Letters

KAF	LAMED	MEN	SAMEKH

Where Did the Bible Come From?

Versions and Paraphrases

Scripture

"All Scripture is given by God and is useful for teaching and for showing people what is wrong in their lives. It is useful for correcting faults and teaching how to live right."   2 Timothy 3:16, ICB

Goal

Learn that the Bible was originally written in Hebrew, Aramaic, and Greek, and that the Bibles we have are translations. There are three basic types of translations: word-for-word, thought-for-thought, and free.

INTRODUCTION *Introduction*

Gather as many different versions and paraphrases of the Bible as you can find. Display them in class. Give each student a piece of plain paper and some crayons. Ask the students to place part of the paper across the title on the front of one of the Bibles and rub over the paper with the crayon to copy the title onto the paper. Ask them to do the same with as many of the other Bibles as they can. Each student's paper should be covered with a variety of textures and letter styles. Ask the students to look at the title pages inside and find out what version each Bible is. Ask them to read Genesis 1:1 from each Bible to see how they are different and how they are alike.

DISCOVERY RALLY *Discovery Rally*

Gather students together in a large group.

WHAT'S THE GOOD WORD?
Choose a student to read the Scripture for today.

THE CHALLENGE
Ask students to name some different languages from around the world.

Ask: **Who knows how to write in a different language?** If someone does, ask him to write in that different language the word that you whisper into his ear. Whisper *day* or *night* or some other simple word.

If the students don't know another language but you do, you may write a word. Ask the other students to try to figure out what the word says. Then tell the students that the Bible was written in different languages. Tell the students that in their Discovery Groups today, they will learn more about how the Bible was written.

PRAYER

DISCOVERY CENTERS *Discovery Centers*

1. TRANSLATING A CODE
Before the session, write the following letters on poster board.

BMM TDSJQUVSF JT HJWFO CZ HPE.

MATERIALS
poster board, marker, paper, pencils

DO: Give each student a piece of paper and a pencil. Ask the students to translate the sentence. After a few minutes, give them the key to figuring out the code: Each letter in the code stands for the letter that comes right before it in the alphabet. Then let them translate the code.

DISCUSS: Explain to the students that what they just did is what translators do. First someone has to figure out what letters the different markings represent. Then they have to know the language and what the different words mean. Some translators tell the meaning of the writing word by word, just as the students were doing in translating the code. Other translators tell us the meaning of whole phrases thought by thought.

Ask: **If you were translating our alphabet code into the thought that it expresses, what could you say?** Allow time for responses. Suggest this answer: "God gives us all the Scriptures in our Bible."

Explain that other translators write in words that we might use today in our newspapers or on TV. These are called free translations or paraphrases. An example of this is: "Every part of Scripture is God-breathed and useful one way or another" from *The Message*.

Ask: **Can all of these Bibles be correct if each contains Scriptures translated differently? If so, how can they all be correct? If not, why not?** You will find that though they may differ in the wording used, most translations are not different in substance or meaning.

2. DIFFERENT ALPHABETS

Before the session, write the Phoenician alphabet on a piece of poster board or make copies of the alphabet for each student.

MATERIALS
Phoenician Alphabet handout (page 20), poster board, marker, pencils, paper

DO: Give each student a piece of paper and a pencil. Ask each student to write her name on the paper using Phoenician letters.

DISCUSS: Tell the students that the Old Hebrew alphabet, which was probably what most of the Old Testament was written in, was nearly the same as the Phoenician alphabet which they are copying now.

If you have time, give each student another piece of paper and ask him to write his name in phonograms. This is one kind of writing that the Egyptians did, and it served as a fun, game-like way to read. Use a picture of something that starts with the same sound as the word you were going to write. For example, cat + apple + rabbit + leaf = Carl.

Tell the students that Moses, who wrote the first five books of the Bible, knew how to read phonograms as well as other kinds of Egyptian writing, because he grew up in Pharaoh's palace. He also learned the way of writing that the Hebrews used, which became the Phoenician alphabet. This is the alphabet he used when he wrote the first five books of the Bible.

Explain that most of the Old Testament was first written in Hebrew. Some of it was written in Aramaic. The New Testament was first written in Greek.

3. ONE VERSE, MANY VERSIONS

Before the session, use index cards or self-stick notes to mark the location of Matthew 5:13 in as many different versions and paraphrases as you can find. Use at least one word-for-word translation (KJV, NASV, or RSV). Use at least one thought-for-thought translation (NIV, NIrV, NAB, NLT, CEV, GNB, JB, NEB, or NCV). Use at least one free translation or paraphrase (Phillips, The Message).

MATERIALS
index cards or self-stick notes, several translations and paraphrases of the Bible, construction paper, glue, alphabet-shaped cereal, bowls

DO: Give one Bible to each student. Ask each student to look on the spine of the Bible to find out what the name of the translation is. Then ask each student in turn to read aloud the name of the translation and the verse you've marked.

DISCUSS: Ask the students the following questions:
- **Which Bible version was the easiest for you to understand?**
- **Which was the most difficult to understand?**
- **How can all the different versions be right if they use different words?**
- **Why do you think there are so many different translations?**

If you have time, give each student a piece of construction paper and glue. Set out several bowls full of alphabet-shaped cereal. Ask the students to glue letters on the paper to spell out, "You are the salt of the earth." Ask them to think about the verse and translate it. In other words, what does it mean?

DISCOVERERS' DEBRIEFING

If you have time to review, gather as a large group and discuss your young discoverers' findings. Ask the following questions:

- **What is the most interesting thing you discovered today?**
- **What is something you learned that you didn't know before?**
- **In what languages was the Old Testament written?**
- **In what language was the New Testament written?**
- **What are the three different kinds of translations?** (word-for-word, thought-for-thought, and free.)
- **Name some of the different translations that people use today.**
- **Can all of these Bibles be correct when they all translate the Scriptures in different ways? If so, how can they all be correct? If not, why not?** (See the note below.)

Review the Scripture for today.

Pray, thanking God for people who translated the Bible from its original languages into words that we can understand.

IMPORTANT: Remind the students to bring empty boxes (the size of cereal boxes, rice boxes, and instant potato boxes) next week. You will need 66 of these boxes for next week's session.

NOTE about translations: Although they may differ in the wording used, most translations are not different in substance or meaning. The differences result from 1) the age of the original manuscripts the translators used (the older the manuscript, the more accurate) and 2) whether the translators are translating word for word, thought for thought, or freely (as in a paraphrase). Differences in translation are the reason it is advisable to study the Bible using several different translations. You may want to show the students the introductions to several translations. This is where the translators tell about how and why they translated the Bible.

Phoenician Alphabet

$\not\prec$ = A

ς = B

7 = G, C

$\triangleleft$ = D

$\overline{\overline{}}$ = E

Y = F, V, U, W, Y

$\mathbb{I}$ = Z

$\mathbb{H}$ = H

$\otimes$ (nothing in English)

7 = I, J

$\mathcal{Y}$ = K

$\langle$ = L

w = M

Y = N

$\mp$ = X

O = O

$?$ = P

ν (nothing in English)

Φ = Q

4 = R

w = S

$+$ = T

Book by Book PART 1

Scripture

"Jesus did many other things as well. If every one of them were written down, I suppose that even the whole world would not have room for the books that would be written." John 21:25

Goal

Learn that there are 66 books in the Bible, 39 in the Old Testament and 27 in the New Testament, and begin learning the names of all the books of the Bible in traditional order.

INTRODUCTION

Set out the 66 boxes you have collected. Give the students paper (plain colors), glue, scissors, and markers. You may use self-stick Con-Tact paper if you prefer. Help the students begin covering the boxes.

DISCOVERY RALLY *Discovery Rally*

Gather students together in a large group.

WHAT'S THE GOOD WORD?
Choose a student to read the Scripture for the day.

THE CHALLENGE
Show the students a book that contains a collection of short stories or fables, or an anthology of some kind.

Ask: **What is the difference is between this kind of book and a book that has chapters in it? Have you ever read a book that had many different stories in it?**

Tell the students that in their Discovery Groups today, they will find out about a book that not only has different stories in it, but also has many different books in it. It is a book of books.

PRAYER

DISCOVERY CENTERS *Discovery Centers*

1. MAKE A LIBRARY

DO: Continue covering the boxes (introductory activity). Explain that each box represents a different book of the Bible. Ask the students to write the name of a book of the Bible on the spine and front of the box book. Students may look at the table of contents in a Bible to see what the names of the books are and how they are spelled.

> **MATERIALS**
> collected boxes, construction paper, glue, scissors, markers, self-stick Con-Tact paper (optional)

DISCUSS: Lead the students to discover that there are 39 books in the Old Testament and 27 books in the New Testament for a total of 66 books in the entire Bible.

Ask: **What are some of the events from the Old Testament? What are some of the events from the New Testament?**

2. A LIBRARY LIST

DO: Give each student a copy of the Bible Library handout. Ask the students to write the name of each book of the Bible in order on the spines of the blank books.

MATERIALS
copies of the Bible Library handout (page 25), pencils

DISCUSS: Ask the students about the book names. **Which book titles are people's names? Which titles are place names?** Ask the students to guess what the other book names mean. The following is a list of the other book names and meanings:

- Genesis means *generation*. Genesis is the book of the generations of the ancient people. Genesis is also used to mean *beginning*.
- Exodus means *exit*.
- Leviticus means *things of the Levites*. The priests were Levites, from the people group of Levi, and Leviticus deals with their jobs or responsibilities.
- Numbers means *numbers* because the people were counted twice.
- Deuteronomy means *second law* because it is the second book that tells about Israel's laws.
- Judges means *judges* because it tells about people who were leaders of God's people and were called judges.
- Kings means *kings* because it tells about the kings of God's people.
- Chronicles means a retelling of history. The students may be able to relate this title to the popular *Chronicles of Narnia*.
- Psalms means poems sung to instrumental music.
- Proverbs means wise sayings.
- Ecclesiastes means *preacher.*
- Acts refers to things the apostles did.
- Revelation means showing things that have not been known before.

Ask the students to write their names at the top of their pages. Keep their pages to use at the Discovery Center next week.

3. CLAP AND SING THE BOOKS OF THE BIBLE

Before the session, practice singing the Books of the Bible songs while you do the pat/clap rhythm. (Tune: *"Ten Little Indians"*)

MATERIALS

copies of the Books of the bible songs handout (page 26)

DO: Group the students into pairs. Ask the partners to face each other, sitting down on the floor or in chairs. Then start a pat/clap rhythm:

- Pats your own legs once.
- Clap your own hands once.
- Clap your right hand to your partner's right hand once.
- Clap your own hands again.
- Clap your left hand to your partner's left hand once.
- Claps your own hands again.
- Clap both of your hands to both of your partner's hands (left hand to partner's right and right hand to partner's left).
- Clap your own hands again.

This ends the sequence. The partners continue this sequence over and over again as they sing. As they learn the Books of the Bible songs and the clapping sequence, challenge them to go faster.

DISCOVERERS' DEBRIEFING

If you have time to review, gather as a large group and discuss your young discoverers' findings. Ask the following questions:

- **What is the most interesting thing you discovered today?**
- **What did you learn that you didn't know before?**
- **How many books are in the Bible?**
- **How many books are in the Old Testament?** (Try to sing the books together.)
- **How many books are in the New Testament?** (Try to sing the books together.)

Review the Scripture for today.

Pray, thanking God for the Old Testament and the New Testament. Ask God to help all of us learn how to find the different books in our Bibles.

Bible Library

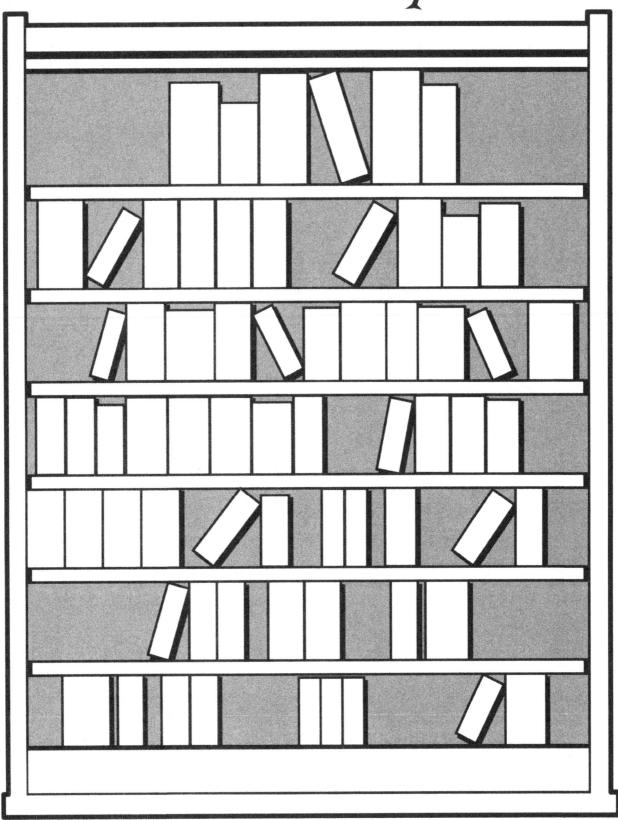

Studying the BIBLE   The foundation for knowing God   25

Books of the Bible
Old Testament

Gen-e-sis, Ex-o-dus, Le-vi-ti-cus, Num-bers, Deut-er-on-o-my, Josh-u-a, Jud-ges, R-uth,

First and Sec-ond Sam-u-el, First and Sec-ond Kin-gs, First and Sec-ond Chron-i-cles.

Ez-ra, Ne-he-mi-ah, Es-ther, Jo-b, Psalms, Pro-verbs, Ec-cle-si-as-tes, Song of Sol-o-

mon, I-sa-iah, Jer-e-mi-ah, Lam-en-ta-tions, E-ze-kel, Dan-iel, Ho-se-a, Jo-el,

A-mos, O-ba-di-ah, Jo-nah, Mi-cah, Na-hum, Ha-bak-kuk,

Zeph-a-ni-ah, Hag-gai, Zech-a-ri-ah, Mal-a-chi.

New Testament

(to the tune of *Skip to My Lou*)

Mat-thew, Mark, Luke, and John, Acts and Ro-mans,

First and Sec-ond Co-rin-thi-ans, Ga-la-tions and E-phe-sians, Phi-

lip-pi-ans, Co-los-sians, First and Sec-ond Thes-sa-lo-ni-ans, First and Sec-ond Tim-o-thy,

Ti-tus, and Phi-le-mon, He-brews, Ja-mes, First and Sec-ond Pe-ter,

First and Sec-ond and Third John, Jude and Rev-e-la-tion.

Book by Book Part 2

Scripture

"The grass withers and the flowers fall, but the word of our God stands forever." Isaiah 40:8

Goal

Learn why the books of the Bible are arranged as they are.

INTRODUCTION

Write the name of the books of the Bible on index cards, one book title per card. As each student arrives, safety-pin one card to the back of the student's shirt without letting the student see the card. Each student must try to guess which book is pinned to his back. The student may get other students to give him clues by asking the other students a question that has a yes or no answer. For example, "Is this book in the Old Testament?" "Is this book named after a person?" "Is the person a man?" If the student quickly guesses the book, or if you want the game to continue for awhile, pin a different card onto the back of his shirt.

DISCOVERY RALLY *Discovery Rally*

Gather the students together in a large group.

WHAT'S THE GOOD WORD?
Choose a student to read the Scripture for the day.

THE CHALLENGE
Show the students the contents page of a Bible.

Say: **The books of the Bible are out of order from the way things really happened. Can you guess why.**

Tell the students that in their Discovery Groups today, they will find out more about how the Bible was written and arranged.

PRAYER

DISCOVERY CENTERS

1. MIXED-UP BOOKS

DO: Make several stacks of the Bible books in random order and time the students to see how quickly they can put all of the books in order, lining them across a table or floor space as if the books were on a shelf.

MATERIALS
Bible books made from boxes during the previous session, timer

DISCUSS: Tell the students that the word *Bible* means *book*. The word *Bible* comes from the Greek word *biblos* which means *book* or *scroll*. **So our Bible is one book, but it is made of many books.**

Ask: **Why do we call the Bible the Word of God? How can we call the Bible God's Word when the different books were written by different people?** Read and discuss 2 Peter 1:21: "Men led by the Holy Spirit spoke words from God" (ICB).

2. GROUPING THE OLD TESTAMENT BOOKS

DO: Give each student his Bible Library that he labeled last week, and distribute the colored pencils. Ask the students to choose one color for the books of the Old Testament that we call Law. Ask them to color the books of Genesis, Exodus, Leviticus, Numbers, and Deuteronomy the color they have chosen for Law books.

> **MATERIALS**
> completed Bible Library handouts (page 25) from Session 3, colored pencils

Ask students to choose a different color for the Old Testament books we call History. Ask them to color the books of Joshua through Esther the color they chose for History books.

Ask students to choose a different color for the Old Testament books we call Poetry. Ask them to color the books of Job through Song of Solomon the color they chose for Poetry books.

Ask students to choose a different color for the Old Testament books we call Major Prophets. Ask them to color the books of Isaiah through Daniel the color they chose for Major Prophets.

Ask students to choose a different color for the Old Testament books we call Minor Prophets. Ask them to color the books of Hosea through Malachi the color they chose for Minor Prophets.

DISCUSS: **Three hundred years before Jesus was born, all the Old Testament books had been written. Many people think that Ezra led the group who chose which books went into what they called the Scriptures. Some people thought that other books should be included. Some of these were Tobit, Judith, Susanna, Bel and the Dragon, Maccabees. In Jesus' time, the books of our Old Testament were the only books of the Bible, the Scriptures, and they were divided into only two parts: the Law and the Prophets. When the Old Testament (originally written in Hebrew and Aramaic) was translated into Greek, the translators arranged the books in the order we have them today, in these five groups. The Major Prophets are called major because those books are longer. The Minor were called minor because those books are shorter.**

If you have time left, sing the books of the Old Testament.

IMPORTANT: Ask the students to take their Bible Library pages with them to Discovery Center #3.

3. GROUPING THE BOOKS OF THE NEW TESTAMENT

DO: Provide your first group with their Bible Library pages from Session 3 (see Discovery Center #2). Subsequent groups will bring their pages with them.

> **MATERIALS**
> completed Bible Library pages from the last session, colored pencils

Tell the students that the New Testament is arranged into three groups: History, Paul's Letters, and Letters from Other Writers. **Note:** Directions for coloring the Bible Library handout are based on these three New Testament divisions. If you prefer Gospels or Biography (4), History (1), Letters (21), and Prophecy (1), instruct your students accordingly.

Ask the students to choose a color for the New Testament books we call History. Ask them to color the books of Matthew through Acts the color they chose for History.

Ask the students to choose a color for Paul's Letters. Ask them to color Romans through Philemon the color they chose for Paul's Letters.

Ask the students to choose a color for Letters from Other Writers. Ask them to color Hebrews through Revelation the color they chose for Letters from Other Writers.

DISCUSS: At first the New Testament books were shared and sent from place to place separately. Little by little they were collected and put together. Then they were copied again and again and sent throughout the Roman Empire. At last (in A.D. 397), a group of church leaders met together and made the official decision to include these books in this order in the Scriptures we call the New Testament.

If you have time, sing the books of the New Testament song. Then hand a Bible to each student. Ask the students to open it up right in the middle and find out which book is at the middle of the Bible. Ask them to find the beginning of the New Testament and notice about where it is located in the whole Bible. Then practice turning to the different books of the Bible. You can call out the name of a book at random (include both New and Old Testament books), and let the students find it in their Bibles. They can hum the books of the Bible to themselves if they want to use the song to help find the book.

DISCUSS: Ask the students to notice that the Bible is divided into chapters and verses. Many Bible experts think that the Scriptures were divided into chapters so that the men who read aloud in the synagogues (Jewish houses of worship) would know where to begin and where to end their reading. The New Testament was divided into chapters soon after all the books were collected together. But these chapters were shorter than the ones we have today. Most Bible experts think that the Archbishop of Canterbury in England made the chapters the way we have them today. The chapters were divided into verses by a French printer in 1551 so that he could make a reference book called a concordance. This French printer did most of his work while he was taking a trip on horseback! The Old Testament chapters were divided into verses soon after that.

DISCOVERERS' DEBRIEFING

If you have time to review, gather as a large group and discuss your young discoverers' findings. Ask the following questions:

- **What is the most interesting thing you discovered today?**
- **What did you learn today that you didn't know before?**
- **Name the five groups of books in our Old Testament.**
- **Name the three groups of books in our New Testament.**
- **How did our Bible come to be arranged in the order we have it now?**
- **If you were arranging the Bible books, would you go in a different order?**
- **If you would have chosen a different order, which book would you have put first? Why?**

Review the Scripture for today.

Pray, thanking God for the Bible. Ask him to help us learn how to find our way to the different books of the Bible so we can study more easily.

Seeking God and His Ways Part 1

Scripture
"You will seek me and find me when you seek me with all your heart." Jeremiah 29:13

Goal
Learn what it means to seek God. Learn that God wants us to seek Him. Learn what blessings come from seeking God.

INTRODUCTION

As students arrive, give each of them a pencil and a copy of the Famous Discoverers' Riddles (pages 37, 38). Ask them to match the discoverer to his discovery or invention.

OPTION: Copy each discoverer's riddle onto an index card. Write the list of discoveries or inventions on a poster board. Keep the poster board hidden. Give each student an index card and challenge the student to figure out what discovery or invention his discoverer made. But the student is not to tell anyone if she figures it out. When all the students are gathered for the Discovery Rally, let each student read aloud the riddle on her index card. The rest of the group tries to guess the discovery or invention that goes with that discoverer. You may show students the list of discoveries and inventions on the poster board, or you may keep it hidden until they need help guessing the correct answer.

ANSWERS: Balboa/Pacific Ocean, Judson/zipper, Walker/match, ancient Egyptians/glass, Birdseye/frozen food, Fleming/penicillin, Franklin/electricity, Bell/telephone, Galileo/telescope, Daguerre/photographs, Hunt/safety pin, Schawlow & Townes/lasers.

DISCOVERY RALLY

Gather students together in a large group.

WHAT'S THE GOOD WORD?

Choose a student to read the Scripture for today.

THE CHALLENGE

If you have chosen the optional introductory activity, do that now.

Say: **Sometimes discoveries come about by accident, but most discoveries and inventions come from someone who was seeking. The discoverers and inventors are looking for something. God wants us to seek him.** Tell the students that in their Discovery Groups today, they are going to learn about seeking God.

PRAYER

DISCOVERY CENTERS

1. HALL OF FAME

Before the session, write on each index card the name of a biblical character who sought God and the Scripture reference that tells about his seeking. Or copy and cut apart Seekers listed on page 36.

> **MATERIALS**
> Seekers (page 36), paper, Bibles, index cards, crayons, markers, colored pencils

DO: Give each student a piece of paper, a Bible, and a prepared index card. Set out crayons, colored markers, or colored pencils. Ask the students to look up and read silently the Scripture reference that tells about their person. Then they should draw an imaginary portrait of that person. At the bottom of the portrait, they should write the person's name and the Scripture reference.

This activity will give students practice in turning to Scriptures in their Bibles. You may need to help them. You may also need to help them read the passage, depending on the student's reading level and the reading level of the Bible the student is using.

DISCUSS: Talk with the students about seeking God. Ask: **Have you ever played Hide and Seek? What does it means to seek? What does it means to seek God?** (It means to wonder about him and try to find out about him and his will.) **What are some ways that we can seek God?** (Prayer, worship, Bible reading, asking older Christians about God.) Tell students that God wants us to seek him.

If you have time, ask each student in the group to show her picture to the rest of the group and tell what happened because the person sought God.

2. A TO Z, WHAT DO YOU KNOW?

DO: Give each student a length of paper tape and a marker, colored pencil, or crayon. Ask students to write the words "God Is" at the top of the tape. Then ask them as a group to describe God with a word that begins with A. All of the students should write the word below "God Is" on the tape. Continue asking for descriptions of God, beginning each new description with the next letter of the alphabet. Use all the letters. (For X you can use a word in which the second letter is X: eXciting, eXpert, and so on.)

MATERIALS
fine-point colored markers, colored pencils, roll of calculator tape cut into 4-foot lengths

DISCUSS: Talk about knowing God. Ask: **What is the difference is between knowing about God and knowing God? Can you serve and follow God and not know him?**

Read 1 Samuel 3:1, 7 and John 5:39, 40 with the students. Ask: **How do we learn *about* God? How do we get to *know* God? What does all this have to do with *seeking* God?**

3. SEEKING FROM THE PSALMS

DO: Group the students into pairs. Give each pair a pencil, a Bible, and a piece of paper. Explain that they are now going to *seek* to learn about God. Assign each pair a psalm. One person in each pair will read the psalm aloud. They will both listen for what it tells them about God. The one who is not reading will

MATERIALS
Bibles, paper, pencils

write down what it says about God. It may be only a name. It may be a description of something God does. It may be a description of who God is. For example, the following descriptions are taken from Psalm 8, ICB:

- God is our Master.
- His name is the most wonderful in all the earth.
- He has taught children and babies to praise him.
- He silences his enemies.
- He has made the heavens with his hands.
- He created the moon and stars.
- He put people in charge of everything he made.

Most psalms can be "mined" like this, but some that are particularly full of descriptions are Psalms 8, 15, 18, 23, 25, 27, 29, 33, 34, 46, 65, 68, 88, 90, 93, 103, 104, 121, 139, 144, and 145.

If you have time, let one student from each pair read the descriptions that they found. If you have even more time, you can assign a second psalm to the pairs.

DISCUSS: Let the students know that they can learn more about God *and* get to know God better by studying the Bible. Ask: **What are some other ways that you can get to know *about* God and to get to *know* God?**

DISCOVERERS' DEBRIEFING

If you have time to review, gather as a large group and discuss your young discoverers' findings. Ask the following questions:
- **What is the most interesting thing you discovered today?**
- **What did you learn that you didn't know before?**
- **What is the difference between knowing *about* God and *knowing* God?**
- **How can we grow in what we know *about* God?**
- **How can we get to *know* God better?**
- **Why does God want us to seek him?**
- **What are some of the blessings we receive when we seek God?**
- **Is there ever a time when we can stop seeking God? Why or why not?**
- **Why will God not let us find out everything there is to know about Him?**

Review the Scripture for today.

Pray, thanking God for allowing us to get to know Him better.

Moses	**Exodus 32:11, 14**
Hannah	**1 Samuel 1:10, 11, 20**
David	**Psalm 34:4–7**
King Jehoahaz	**2 Kings 13:4, 5**
King Asa	**2 Chronicles 14:2, 7**
King Jehoshaphat	**2 Chronicles 17:3–5**
Jonah	**Jonah 2:1, 7–10**
King Uzziah	**2 Chronicles 26:3–5**
Hosea	**Hosea 6:3; 10:12**
King Hezekiah	**2 Chronicles 31:20, 21**
King Manasseh	**2 Chronicles 33:11–13**
King Josiah	**2 Chronicles 34:1–3, 28**
Daniel	**Daniel 6:10, 16, 20–22**
Ezra	**Ezra 7:8–10**
Nicodemus	**John 3:1, 2; 19:38–42**

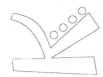

36   Seeking God and His Ways

Famous Discoverers' Riddles

My name is Vasco Balboa. I am from Spain. I was the first person from Europe to discover a huge body of water off the west coast of North and South America. **What did I discover?**

penicillin

My name is Whitcomb Judson. I discovered that I could line up some fasteners, making them stick together, and I could pull them apart using a slider. This slide fastener was used in men's pants first, and later was used in ladies' clothes. **What was this invention that came from my discovery?**

glass

My name is John Walker. I was a pharmacist. In 1827 I discovered that I could put some chemicals on the end of a 3-inch stick. Then I could pull it through a fold of rough paper and it would burst into flame. I called my invention a "congreve." **What do people call one of these today?**

zipper

We lived in ancient Egypt. About 1500 years before Jesus was born, we discovered that we could mix sand, soda, and lime to make a shiny, clear material that we could make into vases and bowls and jars. This material is still used to make vases, bowls, and jars today. **What was the material we discovered?**

frozen food

My name is Clarence Birdseye. In 1925 I discovered that I could keep fish and vegetables from spoiling by lowering the temperature around them. **What invention came about because of my discovery?**

Pacific Ocean

My name is Alexander Fleming. I discovered that I could turn a certain kind of mold into a very powerful medicine. You have probably taken this medicine for sore throats and ear aches. **What did I discover?**

match

My name is Benjamin Franklin. I discovered something very powerful and shocking when I flew a kite in a rainstorm. You use it every day almost everywhere you go. **What did I discover?**

My name is Alexander Graham Bell. In 1876 I discovered that I could say words close to a machine in one room and I could be heard clearly in another room. **What invention came from what I discovered?**

My name is Galileo. In 1609 I discovered that when I looked through a long, heavy tube with glass lenses at each end, the moon, stars and planets looked much larger. I even saw the four moons of Jupiter and the rings of Saturn. **What invention came from what I discovered?**

My name is Louis Daguerre. I am from France. I discovered that I could let light shine on a sheet of copper coated with silver. I could put salt and other chemicals onto this sheet and see a picture on it. **What invention came from my discovery?**

My name is Walter Hunt. In 1849 I discovered that I could take a short, thin, pointed piece of metal and bend it so that it could hold things together, but I hid the point of the metal so people would not get pricked by it. **What invention came from my discovery?**

Our names are Arthur Schawlow and C.H. Townes. We discovered that we could make light shine in one very bright, thin beam. Our research helped Theodore Maiman build a beam so powerful that it can burn a hole in a diamond. Many doctors use it to help repair different parts of the body during surgery. **What did we discover?**

frozen food

photographs

lasers

safety pin

telescope

telephone

Seeking God and His Ways Part 2

Scripture
"Come near to God and he will come near to you."
James 4:8

Goal
Learn some of the ways we can seek God.

INTRODUCTION

Before the session, purchase several rolls of SMARTIES® candies and LIFESAVERS® candies so that there is one roll of candy for each student. Tape each SMARTIES roll on an index card on which you have written, "It's smart to seek God." Tape each LIFESAVERS roll on an index card on which you have written, "Seeking and finding God is like seeking and finding a lifesaver in the sea." Punch a hole in each index card and then tie a string that is about 8 feet long (or longer, depending on the size of your room) through the hole in the card. Hide the cards at various locations in your room with the strings extending out into the center of the room like a web. As each student enters the room, he chooses one string and follows it to the prize at the end. If the students have extra time while they are waiting for others to arrive, ask them to write the names of other kinds of candies on the back of their index cards and try to make up slogans with those names. (Like: "Seek the Creator of the Milky Way®" or "Why was the old man a JOLLY RANCHER™? He found God.")

DISCOVERY RALLY

Discovery Rally

Gather the students together in a large group.

WHAT'S THE GOOD WORD?

Choose a student to read the Scripture for today.

THE CHALLENGE

Ask the students to describe how to play Hide and Seek.

Ask: **Are there different ways to play the game? Have you ever tried to seek God? Does God hide from us when we seek him?**

Then tell the students that in their Discovery Groups today, they will learn more about seeking God.

PRAYER

DISCOVERY CENTERS

Discovery Centers

1. SEEKER BOOKMARKS

Before the session, cut the index cards in half horizontally to make two long rectangles the size of bookmarks.

MATERIALS
large index cards, fine-tipped markers or colored pencils, self-adhesive clear Con-Tact paper

DO: Give one rectangle to each student. These will be bookmarks for their Bibles. Ask the students to write "I am a Seeker" on their bookmarks. Then they can design and color the the bookmarks.

DISCUSS: Ask the students to tell you some ways to seek God. Here are some ways that they might mention or you might suggest.

• Think about God and wonder about him. You can do this anytime, but it is especially easy to do at night when you look at the stars, or when you look at nature: snow, mountains, trees, waterfalls and other things God made.
• Talk to God. You can even ask him about himself.
• Realize God is with you every moment. He walks beside you during the day. He is

beside you as you ride. He is with you as you sleep. See how often you can think of
him during each day.

• Watch for what God is doing around you. Say a "flash prayer": "Thanks, Father."
Or "Great sunset, Lord!"

• Read the Bible to find out what God is like. Also read it to see what God is telling
you. What words or verses seem to shout at you? When you read them, your spirit
says, "Yes!"

• Andrew sought Jesus (John 1:40). He followed Jesus. As he followed Jesus, he got to
know God better. As you follow Jesus, you will also get to know God better. (See
John 14:23.)

Ask the students to write the following words on back of their bookmarks to remind them
of ways to seek God: Wonder, Talk, Pray, Think, Watch, Read, Follow. To make their
bookmarks more durable, let the students cover the bookmarks with clear Con-Tact paper.

2. FOLLOWING CLUES

Before the session, cut apart each clue card hide it in the
location that the previous clue is for. For example, clue #1
tells the students to look under the table. So you will tape
clue #2 to the bottom of the table. Clue #2 tells the students
to look on a pencil. So you will roll the paper containing
clue #3 around a pencil and tape it there. Continue this way until all clues are hidden.
(The last card is not a clue, but a Scripture.)

MATERIALS
copy of Clues (page 44)

DO: Group the students into pairs. The eight clues will be enough to occupy seventeen
students. If you have eight or fewer students, each student may both read and seek. Ask
the students to decide which person in each pair will be the reader and which will be the
seeker.

Say: **When Jesus came, he showed us what God was like. So they will be seeking clues
about God from Jesus' life.**

Give one reader the first clue. This student reads the Scripture and question. After talking
about the question, the student reads the clue aloud. Then the student and his partner try to
guess where the clue is telling them to look. The seeker of the pair goes to find the next
clue at this location. When the seeker finds the clue, the seeker gives it to the next pair.
The reader of this pair reads, the seeker seeks, and so on.

If all of your pairs have read and found clues and there are still some clues hidden, you may save them for the next group. Or if you have time, go through the pairs again until all the clues have been found.

NOTICE: After finding and reading a clue, the student should put the clue back where she found it, so that the clues remain hidden for the next Discovery Center group.

3. SEARCH ENGINES

DISCUSS: Talk about how to find information. Ask: **What is a search engine on the internet?** (A search engine is a way to get information.) Show the students a concordance, a topical index of the Bible, a Bible handbook, a commentary, a Bible atlas, a Bible dictionary, and any other study tool you brought. If you use any of these tools on computer and are able to bring the computer, show these programs to the students.

> **MATERIALS**
> concordance, topical Bible, Bible handbook, Bible commentary, Bible atlas, Bible dictionary, other Bible study tools, paper, pencils

DO: Give one student the concordance. Help this student look up the word *Creator*. Ask another student to count how many times the word *Creator* is used in the Bible. Ask a third student to read the letters in front of each Scripture (Ge, Dt, Ecc, etc.). Ask a fourth student to write these letters on a chalk board or white board so the group can see them. Now ask the group to guess which books of the Bible each of these abbreviations stands for. Finally, ask a fifth student to look up one of the scriptures and read it.

Then ask another student to look up the word *God* in the concordance. Ask this student to count how many pages of Scriptures there are for the word *God*. Ask the students why there are so many.

Give each student a piece of paper and ask each one to write the word *GOD* across the paper in large block letters. Then they should choose one Scripture from the concordance from the book of Psalms (abbreviated Ps) and write that Scripture across the bottom of the paper. They can then design and color the page.

As the students work, introduce them to the other books or programs, showing them how these tools help people seek God.

Discoverers' Debriefing

DISCOVERERS' DEBRIEFING

If you have time to review, gather as a large group and discuss your young discoverers'
findings. Ask the following questions:

- **What is the most interesting thing you discovered today?**
- **What did you learn today that you didn't know before?**
- **Name some ways we can seek God.**
- **If you could ask God anything, what would it be?**
- **Name some of the things that we learn about God by reading about Jesus' life.**
- **What are some of the "search engines" or tools that help people find out about God?**

Review the Scripture for today.

Pray, thanking God for allowing us to get to know him better. Thank him for the tools that
people have made to help us learn more about him.

CLUES

1. Read John 1:18.
    What does this tell you about God?

    I'm a place to work,
    I'm a place to eat.
    But under me
    All I can see are your feet.

2. Read John 2:23-25.
    What does this tell you about God?

    I make my mark,
    And I know you're glad
    When you want to draw
    On your drawing pad.

3. Read John 6:5-13.
    What does this tell you about God?

    I stand here every week
    Holding lots of books.
    But today you'll find a clue on me
    If anybody looks!

4. Read Matthew 19:13, 14.
    What does this tell you about God?

    The sun comes in.
    You look out.
    Is there a clue near me?
    You'll find out!

5. Read Mark 10:46-52.
    What does this tell you about God?

    We have backs and feet.
    But people sit on us; it's true.
    And under one of us
    You will find a clue.

6. Read Matthew 13:54-56.
    What does this tell you about God?

    Take a look inside a book
    That you're here to study about.
    When you do, you'll find a clue.
    Read it and figure it out.

7. Read Mark 2:1-12
    What does this tell you about God?

    Think about it.
    You'll never believe
    What your teacher
    Has up her sleeve!

8. Read Mark 4:36-41.
    What does this tell you about God?

    For a clue
    That can't be beat,
    Look on the floor
    Where two walls meet.

CLUE ANSWERS
1. table
2. pencil
3. shelf
4. window
5. chair
6. Bible
7. up your sleeve
8. in a corner

9. Read John 3:16.
    What does this tell you about God?

Study by Topics

Scripture

"[Moses] said to them: 'Pay attention to all the words I have said to you today. Command your students to obey carefully everything in these teachings. These should not be unimportant words for you. They mean life for you!"
Deuteronomy 32:46, 47, ICB

Goal

Learn that one way to study the Bible is to look for what it says about certain topics. Learn to use a simple concordance and/or topical index of the Bible.

INTRODUCTION

In preparation for using the concordance or topical index, have students practice alphabetizing. Write each of the following animal names on an index card, with each column of animals written on a different color of card.

ape	aardvark	anteater
bear	buffalo	beaver
crocodile	cougar	cow
duck	dinosaur	donkey
elephant	eel	emu

flamingo	ferret	fox
gnu	giraffe	gazelle
hare	hippopotamus	horse
ibis	impala	iguana
jaybird	june bug	jackrabbit
kangaroo	katydid	koala
lion	lynx	llama
mouse	monkey	mule
nighthawk	nightingale	newt
ostrich	octopus	owl
pig	platypus	parrot
quetzal	queen bee	queen ant
raccoon	robin	rat
seal	sheep	spider
turtle	toad	toucan
urchin	umbrella bird	unicorn
vole	vulture	viper
walrus	worm	whale
x-ray fish	yak	zebra

Mix the cards up. As each student arrives, give each one five cards and ask her to arrange them in alphabetical order. The students' ability to alphabetize will vary according to their age and experience. Ask another teacher or aide in your classroom to assist the students who need help. When the student is finished, she returns the cards to you, and you give the student another set of five.

If you have enough students, divide them into three groups and give each group a set of cards that are the same color, but mixed alphabetically. Ask each group to arrange their cards in alphabetical order.

DISCOVERY RALLY Discovery Rally

Gather the students together in a large group.

WHAT'S THE GOOD WORD?

Choose a student to read the Scripture for today.

THE CHALLENGE

Show the students an empty box. Ask them to imagine that the box holds information about transportation. Ask: **What do you think of when you say** *transportation.* When they say the thing they think about, they should also pretend to throw it into the box. You pretend to catch it with the box. You can do the same with the word *seasons* or the word *Christmas.*

Say: **The words you said are topics. That means that there are many things that relate to that word. A topic is like a box. Many things go with a topic.** Explain that in their Discovery Groups today, they will find out how to learn what the Bible says about different topics.

PRAYER

Discovery Centers

DISCOVERY CENTERS

1. NATIONAL THEOGRAPHIC

MATERIALS
yellow loose-leaf report folder for each student, light blue construction paper cut into 7-by-10-inch pieces, markers, colored pencils, crayons, pencils

DISCUSS: Introduce the activity. Ask: **Have you ever heard of the magazine called** *National Geographic?* **What is geography?** *Graph* means *writing.* *Geo* means *earth.* **So geography or geographic means writing about the earth.** Tell the students they will make a folder today that will be their own private magazine, *National Theographic.* Explain that *theo* means *God.* Ask: **What do you think theographic might mean?**

DO: Give each student a yellow loose-leaf report folder. (If the students came to you from another center, ask them to put their papers from the previous center into the folder.) Then give each student a piece of pre-cut light blue construction paper. Ask them to glue the blue paper onto the front of the folder so that the yellow folder shows as a border around the paper. Give each student a copy of the title. The pattern follows this activity description. Tell the students to glue this onto the blue paper. They can design and draw a cover illustration on the blue paper. You may ask them to suggest as a group some of the different kinds of pictures they might draw. If they need help, suggest that they write some of the descriptions of God they used in Session 5, Discovery Center #2. Or they might draw a rainbow (God's promises), a tree and landscape (God's creation), a cloud (the way God led the Israelites). Or they could simply color an abstract design.

DISCUSS: As the students work, talk about seeking God. Ask: **Have you sought God this week? How? Did God teach you anything this week?** Tell them something you learned about God this week. If you have time left, show them some topical indexes in the back of some Bibles and let them practice looking up topics.

Your group will need to take their folders with them to the next center. If this is the last group, keep their folders for next session.

NATIONAL THEOGRAPHIC

2. THEOGRAPHIC REPORTERS

DO: Give each student a pencil and piece of notebook paper. Also give each student a Bible that has a topical index in back. (Option: Give one student a topical index or concordance and give another student a Bible. This is a good option if some of your students have difficulty reading, or if you don't have enough Bibles available.) In addition, you may bring small electronic concordances or a computer with a concordance installed in it, if you have these. Tell the students that they are going to be reporters for the *National Theographic*, so they will write an article to go into their "magazine."

MATERIALS
Bibles with a topical index, pencils, notebook paper

Ask the students to look at the topical index in the back of their Bible. Ask them what kinds of topics it tells about. Now ask them to write "Love" as the title on their papers. Next they should look up "love" in the index of their Bible. Tell them to choose one of the Scriptures listed, turn to that Scripture, and copy it onto the paper. Suggest Scriptures from Psalms, Proverbs, John, 2 Corinthians, and 1 John.

If only one student has the index or concordance, ask that student to find a Scripture reference, and ask the student with the Bible to look it up and read it aloud so the group can copy it. The students can also look up the topic on the electronic concordance or computer if you have it.

Do three Scriptures on love and then give each student another piece of paper. Ask them to write "Self-Control" as the title. Ask them to look this word up and write some Scriptures that tell about self-control.

If you have time, let students suggest subjects to look up. If they have folders, they should put their pages in the folders. If they don't yet have folders, they should take their pages with them in preparation for making their folders.

If this is the last group, keep their folders for the next class session.

3. GOD'S WORD FOR TODAY

DO: Give each student a magazine to look at. These could even be old issues of *National Geographic*. Ask the students to look through their magazines and find something about which they could ask God, "What do you think of this?"

> **MATERIALS**
> magazines appropriate for your students (remove inappropriate articles and/or ads if needed), notebook paper, glue, pencils

Give each student a piece of notebook paper. Have each student cut out the picture or article that inspired the question and glue or tape it to the paper. Then guide the students to put their question into a word that they could find in their topical index or concordance. You may need to anticipate students's responses, if you think they might want to try to find something that couldn't possibly be in the index. For example, if they say "television," challenge them to think of related words like eyes, see, vision, sight. Then look up those words in the concordance or index. Psalms, Proverbs, the gospels, and the Letters often contain Scriptures that would apply. David said, "I will refuse to look at anything vile and vulgar" (Psalm 101:3, NLT).

Then ask the students to write the Scripture reference they found under the picture or article they taped onto their paper. Ask them to place the paper in their folder if they've made one, or to take it with them to the next group in preparation for making the folder. If this is the last group, keep their folders for next session.

DISCOVERERS' DEBRIEFING

If you have time to review, gather as a large group and discuss your young discoverers' findings. Ask the following questions:

- **What is the most interesting thing you discovered today?**
- **What did you learn today that you didn't know before?**
- **What tool did we use today to learn more about God?**
- **Why might a person use a concordance or index?**
- **How do you use a concordance or index?**
- **Do you have a concordance or index at home?**
- **Do you have a Bible or several Bibles at home? Where would you look in these Bibles to find out if they have indexes or not?** (If a student does not have a Bible at home, give the student a Bible.)

Review the Scripture for today.

Pray, thanking God for different tools like concordances and indexes that help us find out more about him and his Word.

Character Study

Scripture
"That which was from the beginning, which we have heard, which we have seen with our eyes, which we have looked at and our hands have touched—this we proclaim concerning the Word of life." 1 John 1:1

Goal
Learn how to study about a character. Learn how to apply the lessons of Bible characters to our lives.

INTRODUCTION *Introduction*

Make character and partner cards by writing each person's name from the list on page 52 onto an index card. Hide the partner cards in your room. As the students arrive, tell them that they will be learning how to study Bible characters today, but first they'll play a partner matching game. Give each student one character card. Tell them to look at the name on the card and think of who that person's partner is or was. Ask them to hunt for the partner card that is hidden in the room.

When the student finds the partner card, the student takes the two cards to an assistant or teacher who puts this student in a group with at least three other students. The assistant then instructs the students to mix all their cards together and lay them face down in rows. Then one person turns over two cards at random. If the cards are of a character and its partner, the student gets to keep those cards and turn over two more. If they do not match (character with partner) the student turns them face down, and it's another student's turn.

Character and Partner: Tarzan and Jane, Batman and Robin, C3PO and R2D2, Christopher Robin and Winnie-the-Pooh, Calvin and Hobbes, Charlie Brown and Snoopy, Garfield and Odie, Robin Hood and Little John, Big Bird and Elmo, Kermit and Miss Piggy, Lady (the dog) and Tramp (the dog), Snow White and Prince Charming, Beauty and The Beast, Bob (from VeggieTales) and Larry, Ramona and Beezus, Hansel and Gretel, Jack and Jill, Mickey Mouse and Minnie Mouse, Donald Duck and Daisy Duck, Tweedledee and Tweedledum, Burt and Ernie, Doug and Pork Chop.

DISCOVERY RALLY

Gather the students together in a large group.

WHAT'S THE GOOD WORD?

Choose a student to read the Scripture for today.

THE CHALLENGE

Ask: **Who do you think are the most famous partners from the group you just matched?** There will probably be disagreement, and that's all right. **How would find out more about these different characters?** Tell the students that in their Discovery Groups today, they will learn how to find out about Bible characters.

Ask: **What name (besides God and Jesus) do you think is most often mentioned in the Bible?** It's David. His name is in the Bible 1,118 times. Moses is in the Bible 804 times. Saul is talked about 388 times. Aaron's name is mentioned 339 times. And Abraham's name is in the Bible 307 times. Those are the top five names in the Bible.

Give the students their *National Theographic* folders which they made last week. They will add pages to this folder today.

PRAYER

DISCOVERY CENTERS

1. WHO'S MY PARTNER?

Before the session, copy the pages from a concordance that list references for the following names:

Paul	Andrew	James
Sapphira	Adam	Daniel
Rachel	Delilah	Ruth
David	Joshua	Rebekah
Deborah	Baruch	Jezebel
Martha	Aquila	Barnabas

DO: Give each student a piece of notebook paper and a pencil. Ask the students to write the above names in a column on the left hand side of the paper as you read and spell the names for them.

Then give each student the concordance reference page(s) for one or more of the people listed. Ask them to read down the list of Scripture references until they find one that links that person's name and another person's name. This will probably be the person who can be considered the partner. The students may have to look up the reference if they are not certain. Then ask the students to take turns telling the name of the partner, and the other students write this name next to the partner's name on the list. (If you think this will be too difficult for your students, go through the copied pages before class and use a highlighter pen to mark the lines where the character's name is connected to his or her partner's name.)

DISCUSS: Tell the students that this is one way to learn about Bible characters. Ask if they know what the partners did together. If they don't, help them turn to the reference in their Bible and read what it tells them.

The students should add this page to their *National Theographic* folders.

2. WHO AM I?

Before the session, from a good Bible dictionary, photocopy the articles that tell about the following people: Sarai, Silas, Luke, Hannah, Jonathan, Baruch, Deborah, Naomi, Boaz, Elisabeth, Martha, Stephen, Matthew, Candace, Nathanael.

MATERIALS
Bible dictionary, notebook paper, pencils

DO: Show the students the Bible dictionary. Show them how they would find information about a person by looking up his name. But also tell them that some people had the same name. There are five different Marys in the Bible. There are five Johns, five Jameses, and more than twenty Nathans!

Give each boy a photocopied article about a man from the above list. Try to give each girl an article about a woman. Also give the students notebook paper and pencils. Ask them to write the name of the person from their article at the top of the page as the title. Then they should read the article. If students have difficulty reading, they can work in pairs, or you can help by reading the articles to them. You can work as a large group if you wish. The students should write down descriptions of the person on their papers. These can be in the form of a list of one-word descriptions, or they can be written as if the student were describing the person to a friend in a letter. When students are finished, they should put the pages into their folders.

If you have time, the students can take turns telling the group what they found out about the person whose life they researched.

3. LIFE LESSONS

DO: Give each student a piece of notebook paper on which you have written a Bible person's name and a Scripture reference as recommended below. Each reference locates a portion of Scripture that tells something that happened in that person's life.

MATERIALS
notebook paper, pencils, colored pencils

Tell the students that the lives of Bible characters have much to teach us about our lives today. Ask the students to read the reference and then write down 1) what it tells him about that person, and 2) what it teaches him about his own life. Ask: **Is that person someone to follow in attitude, or someone not to follow?**

If you have time, let the students tell each other what they found out. They can even draw a picture of the story, or of what they think that person might have looked like. These pages should be added to their folders.

Martha–Luke 10:38-42	Nehemiah–Nehemiah 2:1-6
Elijah–1 Kings 19:9-18	King Uzziah–2 Chronicles 26:1-5, 16
Herod–Acts 12:18-25	Ruth–Ruth 2:17-23; 4:13-17
Samuel–1 Samuel 16:4-13	Daniel–Daniel 6:6-21
David–1 Samuel 26:6-25	Paul and Silas–Acts 16:16-35
David–1 Samuel 17:32-50	A boy–John 6:5-13
Miriam–Exodus 2:1-10	A girl–2 Kings 5:1-14

DISCOVERERS' DEBRIEFING:

If you have time to review, gather as a large group and discuss your young discoverers' findings. Ask the following questions:

- **What is the most interesting thing you discovered today?**
- **What did you learn today that you didn't know before?**
- **Name some tools we can use to learn about people from the Bible.**
- **Why did God give us these stories about people?**
- **How can we learn lessons from them that apply to our lives today?**

Ask the students to leave their folders with you so they'll be available next week.

Review the Scripture for today.

Pray, thanking God for the Bible and the stories of people and the choices they made. Ask God to help us make the right choices in our lives.

Places and Times

Scripture

"Heaven and earth will pass away, but my words will never pass away."   Mark 13:31

Goal

Learn how to study about Bible places and Bible times.

INTRODUCTION

As students arrive, pin on each student's back a slip of paper which has a location written on it. For example: Disneyland, the Grand Canyon, Mexico, Florida, the Rocky Mountains, the Mississippi River, and so on. Or you may write place names from your own locality if you prefer. Tell the students to ask each other, "Where am I?" The student who is asked may answer with only one clue. Then the one who asked may guess. If she guesses incorrectly, she goes to another student and asks, "Where am I?" If the student who's asked gives a clue that's already been given, then he may give a second clue.

DISCOVERY RALLY

Gather the students together in a large group.

WHAT'S THE GOOD WORD?
Choose a student to read the Scripture for the day.

THE CHALLENGE
Show the students a map of your state and how a Bible times map. Choose maps that have mileage keys at the bottom. (The Bible times maps can be found at the back of many Bibles or in some Bible reference books.) Mark the mileage from the map keys on the edge of an index card and let students measure distances from the Bible times map, then measure that same distance from your town on your state map to find out how far that would be in terms of the area you live in. For example, it was only about 250 miles (straight) from where the Israelites were captive in Egypt to where they entered the promised land. That is only a bit farther than the distance you would travel from Nashville to Memphis. How far is it in your state?

Tell the students that in their Discovery Groups today, they will learn how to find out about Bible places and times.

PRAYER

DISCOVERY CENTERS

1. THE DIG
Before the session, write on the cardboard cylinder: "King Cyrus allows the captives to return home." Make a paper scroll using an index card rolled up and secured with string or a rubber bank. Put a 1-inch layer of dirt or sand in one of the buckets. Then add the following items in this order: coin, layer of dirt, small aluminum foil scroll, layer of dirt, ring, layer of dirt, cardboard cylinder, layer of dirt, small toy boat, layer of dirt, paper scroll, layer of dirt.

MATERIALS
two buckets (used for water when mopping), dirt or sand (or shredded newspaper or popcorn), a coin, small scroll made from aluminum foil, ring, cardboard cylinder (toilet paper roll), small toy boat, paper scroll (index card and string), plastic drop cloth (or something to protect the floor)

DO: Bring the full bucket and the empty bucket to class. You may want to cover the floor at your center with a plastic drop cloth like painters use. Remind the students what an archaeologist does. Then let students be archaeologists and take turns scooping dirt out of the full bucket, putting it into the empty bucket. When a student finds an object, stop and tell the students about the real archaeological finds that these represent.

The **paper scroll** represents the Dead Sea scrolls found in a cave. There were parts of every Old Testament book found except the book of Esther. The whole book of Isaiah was found. It turned out to be the oldest manuscript of Isaiah that had ever been found. Ask a student to read Isaiah 29:11-13.

The **boat** represents an ancient boat that was found in the Sea of Galilee. That boat came from the time when Jesus lived. It is like the boats in which Jesus and his friends would have ridden to cross the lake. Ask a student to read Matthew 9:1.

The **cardboard tube** represents a clay cylinder that was found. This cylinder had writing on it explaining that King Cyrus would allow all captives (which God's people were) to return home and build the temple again. Ask a student to read Ezra 1:2-4.

The **ring** represents a recent archaeological find: Baruch's signet ring. He would have used it to show that his writings were truly his own by stamping the seal of the ring into wax or clay. Ask a student to read Jeremiah 32:13-15.

The **foil scroll** represents two small silver scrolls that were found. Part of the Scripture found in Numbers 6:24-26 was written on them. Ask a student to read Numbers 6:24-26.

The **coin** represents a coin that archaeologists found which has some of the events of the story of Noah's ark shown on it. It also has on it the Greek word *kibotos*, which means *ark*. It was found in a place near the area where Noah's ark would have landed. Ask a student to read Genesis 8:3, 4.

2. THE TIME LINE

DO: Give the students the Time Line pages and help them tape the pages end to end in order. Then give each student a piece of notebook paper. Help the students to tape the left edge of the Time Line onto the center of the paper, fold

MATERIALS
copies of the Time Line (pages 61-67), tape, notebook paper, colored pencils

their Time Lines in accordion folds, and put this page into their *National Theography* folders to form a fold-out.

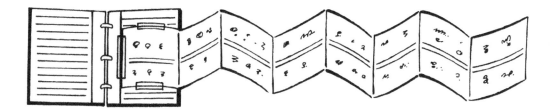

Then ask the students to look at the first section of the time line. With a good Bible dictionary or Bible handbook, help one student look up *ark*. Try to find a drawing of the ark to show the group. (Or you can use a computer program to help with this research if you have a computer available.) Now ask a student to look up *Babel*. This article may refer to *ziggurats*, so look up *ziggurat* and show this picture to the group. Other subjects to look up for the time line are:

- bow and arrow (page 1 of the time line)
- Jericho (page 2)
- Ninevah (page 3)
- temples, pagan (page 5)
- house (page 7)
- tabernacle (page 2)
- Solomon's temple, or temple (page 2)
- scroll (page 4)
- coins (page 6)

The students may want to look up other topics. Feel free to follow their interest. The students may color their Time Lines with colored pencils if you have time after researching these subjects, or while researching these subjects.

(You may find different subjects pictured in your Bible dictionary. The reference materials used for this session are *Holman Bible Dictionary*, Holman Bible Publishers and *Wilmington's Bible Handbook*, Tyndale House Publishers. This Time Line was taken from *Day By Day Kid's Bible*, a chronological retelling of the Bible, paraphrased at a second-grade reading level.)

3. MAP IT OUT

Before the session, punch holes on the left side of each student's maps so they'll fit in the folders.

DO: Display the world map or globe. Ask the students to find the place where they live. Help them find some Bible places on this world map: Egypt, Israel, Greece, Italy. Then give each student a copy of Map of King David's Time, Map of Jesus' Time, Map of Where Paul Traveled, and a Bible. Ask the students to find the maps in the backs of the Bibles. Help them locate places on the maps in their Bibles that will help them fill in the few blanks on the photocopied maps. Then ask the students to follow the directions at the bottom of each map.

MATERIALS
world map or globe, copies of the maps (pages 68-70) for each student, Bibles, colored pencils

The students may color the maps with colored pencils if they have time.

DISCOVERERS' DEBRIEFING:

If you have time to review, gather as a large group and discuss your young discoverers' findings. Ask the following questions:

- **What is the most interesting thing you discovered today?**
- **What did you learn today that you didn't know before?**
- **How can we find out about the land and the people who lived in Bible times?**
- **What are some ways they were different from us?**
- **What are some ways they were like us?**

Say: **Times may have changed, but there's something very important that never changes.** Ask a student to read Hebrews 13:8. Ask another student to read Malachi 3:6. Ask a third student to read James 1:17. Say: **Name something about God that you are glad never changes.**

Review the Scripture for today.

Pray, thanking God for teaching us about the land and times of the Bible, and for also choosing to work in our land and our time today.

When the World Was New

Abraham and His Family

BIBLE

BIBLE

Adam and Eve

Noah

Tower of Babel

Abraham travels

Isaac and Rebekah

Jacob and Esau

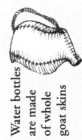

Joseph goes to Egypt

Joseph becomes a ruler in Egypt

WORLD

AROUND 2400 B.C.

Chariots are pulled by donkeys in Sumeria

The Great Sphinx and Cheops' Pyramid are built in Egypt

Dogs are first tamed in Egypt

Games in Egypt: tug-of-war, tossing leather balls stuffed with grain

AROUND 1890 B.C.

Mummies are made in Egypt

People first keep chickens in Babylon

Fighting is done with bows and arrows

Water bottles are made of whole goat skins

First trumpets are made in Denmark

Horses are used to pull carts

From Egypt to the Promised Land

Enemies, Judges, & Kings

A GOOD KING
A GOOD KING PART OF THE TIME

A BAD KING

Baby Moses is born

God's people leave Egypt

Ten rules and a worship tent

Jericho falls

Gideon, Samson, Ruth

Saul, the First King

David, the Singing King

Solomon, the Rich King, builds the worship house

AROUND 1500 B.C.

AROUND 1000 B.C.

First Chinese dictionary

A song in Egypt talks about the Israelites, God's people

Strong ships are built close to the seas

Silk cloth is made in China

The Sun Pyramid is built in Mexico

Cloth is colored with purple dye from snails around the big sea near Israel

People like to shoot slingshots at targets

2

Messages about Kings, Armies, and Idols

	A GOOD KING
	A GOOD KING PART OF THE TIME
	A BAD KING

Bad Kings

PROPHETS

| Elijah | Elisha | Obadiah | Joel | Jonah | Amos |

ISRAEL'S KINGS

| Jeroboam | Nadab | Baasha | Elah | Omri | Ahab | Ahaziah | Joram | Jehu | Jehoahaz | Jehoash | Jeroboam the 2nd |

JUDAH'S KINGS

| Rehoboam | Asa | Jehoshaphat | Jehoram | Queen Athaliah | Joash | Amaziah | Uzziah |

The kingdom of God's people becomes two kingdoms: Israel and Judah

AROUND 930 B.C.

AROUND 790 B.C.

Pinto Indians build huts of wood and reeds in California

Greek stories are written: "Iliad" and "Odyssey"

A favorite sport: hunting from chariots

Favorite foods: camel's milk, roasted locusts, sheep's tails, pomegranate juice

In China and Babylon, people study stars and the way planets move

Singers travel from town to town

First Olympic games: horse racing, wrestling, boxing, and running; women not allowed to come

City of Rome is started

A favorite game in Europe: horseshoes

Messages about What's Coming

	A GOOD KING
	A GOOD KING PART OF THE TIME
	A BAD KING

PROPHETS

Hosea   Micah   Isaiah   Nahum   Zephaniah   Jeremiah   Habakkuk

ISRAEL'S KINGS

Zechariah   Menahem   Pekah   Hoshea

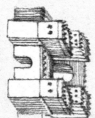

ISRAEL IS TAKEN CAPTIVE BY THE ASSYRIANS (722 B.C.)

JUDAH'S KINGS

Jotham   Ahaz   Hezekiah   Manasseh   Josiah   Jehoahaz   Jehoiakim   Zedekiah

AROUND 750 B.C.   **AROUND 600 B.C.**

Water clocks are used in Assyria to tell time

In Greece, people like songs about fights and wars

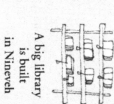

A big library is built in Nineveh

Nebuchadnezzar is king in Babylon

Babylon defeats Assyria (605 b.c.)

NOTE ABOUT THE BIBLE PROPHETS AND KINGS:

Most of the names are on this time line. But some prophets and kings were not around very long. So you won't see their names here.

PROPHETS

 Daniel  Ezekiel  Zechariah  Haggai  Malachi

Judah is taken captive by the Babylonians (605, 597, & 586 B.C.)

Jerusalem is torn down

Maybe the book of Job was written at this time

Zerubbabel leads God's people back to Jerusalem (538 b.c.)

The worship house in Jerusalem is built again

Esther becomes a queen in Persia

Ezra leads more of God's people back home

Nehemiah helps build the wall of Jerusalem back up

AROUND 590 B.C.

AROUND 450 B.C.

Aesop's fables are told

Some children's games: hopscotch, leapfrog, hide-and-seek, tug-of-war

Babylon is overthrown by Persia, and Cyrus becomes king (539 b.c.)

A ship sails around Africa for the first time

In Persia, men riding horses carry messages back and forth like mail

Dams are built in India

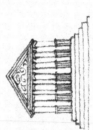

Alexander the Great begins ruling in Greece

Greek people study plants and make medicines from them

There are many plays in Greece, and many temples are built for fake gods

Pigeons are used to carry messages in Greece

The Life of Jesus

The Old Testament is written in Greek

When God's Son came

Jesus teaches and does wonders

Jesus' best gift

AROUND 250 B.C.

AROUND A.D. 30

Greeks rule the country where God's people live

The first Roman coins are made

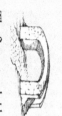

Romans and Greeks play ball games, dice games, games on game boards

The Great Wall of China is built, 1,400 miles long

Paper is first made in China

The first stone bridge is built in Rome

Streets are first paved in Rome

Rome rules the world

Herod the Great is put in charge of the country where God's people live

Greeks and Romans like chariot races

Storytellers travel from town to town

God's Kingdom Grows

AROUND A.D. 30

Peter and John teach, Stephen and Philip preach

Paul travels

Letters from Paul

James, Jude, and Peter write letters

John writes about the future

The Romans learn to use soap

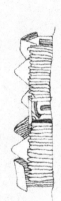

The city of London is started

Nero becomes ruler of Rome

AROUND A.D. 90

Jerusalem and the worship house are torn down

NOTE ABOUT THIS TIME LINE:

The number of years between the pictures is not always the same. There are more than 100 years between some of the pictures at the beginning. There are only a few years between some of the pictures at the end.

MAP OF KING DAVID'S TIME

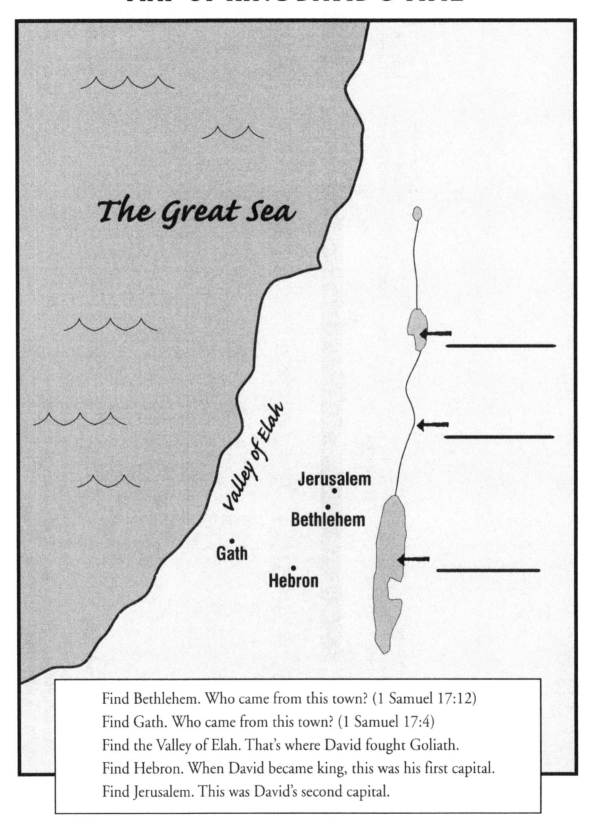

The Great Sea

Valley of Elah

Jerusalem

Bethlehem

Gath

Hebron

Find Bethlehem. Who came from this town? (1 Samuel 17:12)

Find Gath. Who came from this town? (1 Samuel 17:4)

Find the Valley of Elah. That's where David fought Goliath.

Find Hebron. When David became king, this was his first capital.

Find Jerusalem. This was David's second capital.

MAP OF JESUS' TIME

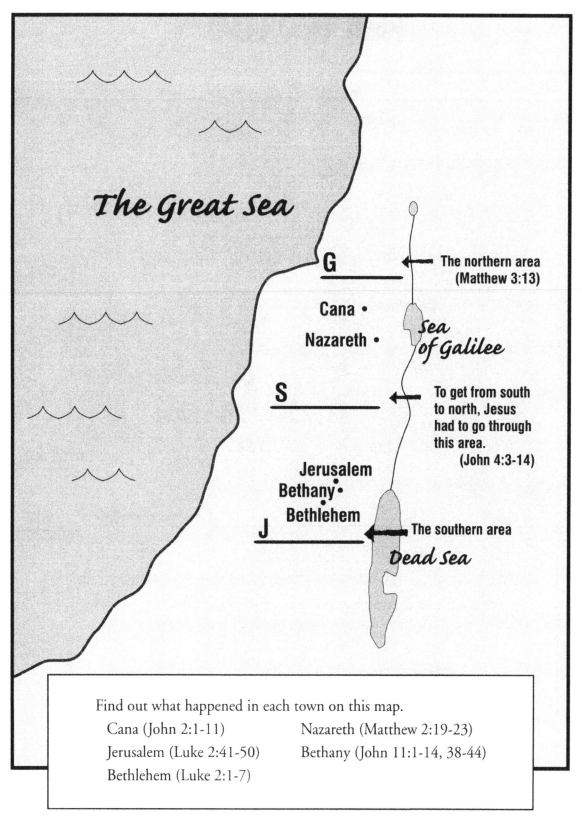

The Great Sea

G — The northern area (Matthew 3:13)

Cana •
Nazareth •

Sea of Galilee

S — To get from south to north, Jesus had to go through this area. (John 4:3-14)

Jerusalem •
Bethany •
Bethlehem •

J — The southern area

Dead Sea

Find out what happened in each town on this map.
Cana (John 2:1-11)   Nazareth (Matthew 2:19-23)
Jerusalem (Luke 2:41-50)   Bethany (John 11:1-14, 38-44)
Bethlehem (Luke 2:1-7)

Studying the BIBLE   The foundation for knowing God

MAP OF WHERE PAUL TRAVELED

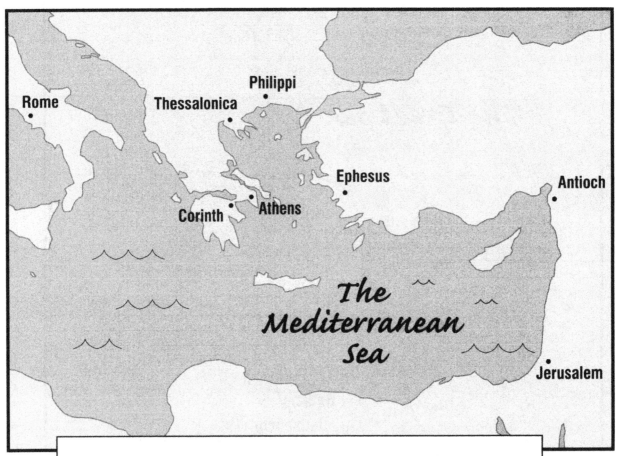

Look in the Table of Contents in your Bible. In the list of New Testament books you will see some of the letters that Paul wrote. Which cities on the map received letters from Paul? How can you tell?

What important thing happened in Antioch? (Acts 11:26) Find Antioch on this map.

Synoptic and Chronological Bibles

Scripture

"The Lord's teachings are perfect, They give new strength.
The Lord's rules can be trusted. They make plain people wise.
The Lord's orders are right. They make people happy.
The Lord's commands are pure. They light up the way.
They are worth more than gold, even the purest gold.
They are sweeter than honey, even the finest honey."
  Psalm 19:7, 8, 10 ICB

Goal

Learn that there are different ways to order the books of the Bible.

INTRODUCTION

As the students arrive, give each student an index card on which you have written the Jewish name of a month, with our corresponding month written in parentheses below it. (See the list on page 72.) Depending on the number of students you have in class, you may need to make two or more of each card so that each student can have one.

Give each student a piece of plain paper and a colored marker or crayon. Ask the students to copy the Jewish name of the month at the bottom of the page and then draw and color a picture that could be used in a calendar for that month.

Nisan	(March–April)	Iyyar	(April–May)
Sivan	(May–June)	Tammuz	(June–July)
Ab	(July–August)	Elul	(August–September)
Tishri	(September–October)	Marcheshvan	(October–November)
Chislev	(November–December)	Tebeth	(December–January)
Shebat	(January–February)	Adar	(February–March)

DISCOVERY RALLY

Gather students together in a large group. Gather their calendar pages in the order listed above. Later you may 1) staple the pages like a book and display the book in class, 2) hang all pictures in order of the months in your classroom or hall to display the students's pictures, or 3) photocopy the book during the coming week so each student can take a copy of it home next week.

WHAT'S THE GOOD WORD?
Choose a student to read the Scripture for today.

THE CHALLENGE
Tell the students that at first, God's people simply used numbers for months, or they used Canaanite names, such as Abib, Ziv, Ehanim, and Bul, all referred to in the Old Testament. After the Jews returned from Babylonian exile, they used month names like those used in the introductory activity. Those month names came from Babylonian names. Explain that the Jewish year did not begin in January. Ask: **Which month do you think began the Jewish year?** It was Nisan (March–April). Ask: **Why do you think that was considered the beginning of the year?** (Because that's when spring started and plants began to bud, bloom, and grow.) Tell the students that in their Discovery Groups today, they will learn about Bibles in which the books are not arranged in the same order as most other Bibles.

PRAYER

DISCOVERY CENTERS

1. SEEING TOGETHER

Before the session, find a synoptic version or harmony of the Gospels. *Synopsis of the Four Gospels*, United Bible Societies, is one resource.

DO: Ask the students to look straight at you and not at each other. Say the name of one student in your group. Ask the rest of the students to tell you what that student is wearing and what color that student's eyes are. Ask: **Does everyone agree? Sometimes we don't notice or remember everything we see, even though we all saw the same thing.**

Tell the students that the word *synoptic* means *seeing together*. **We all saw the same things, but we described these things differently. Matthew, Mark, Luke and John all saw many of the same things that Jesus did, but each one of them wrote these things in different ways.**

Show the students a synoptic version of the Gospels. Sometimes it's called a harmony of the Gospels. Turn to the story of Jesus feeding the five thousand people (Matthew 14:13-21; Mark 6:30-44; Luke 9:10-17; and John 6:1-14). As you read the stories aloud, ask the students to listen for what's the same and what's different in the four tellings.

DISCUSS: Why would there be some differences? Many people think that Mark wrote his book first, remembering what Peter had told him about being with Jesus. Matthew and Luke were able to read Mark's book. So their books are much like Mark's, except for other information they added on their own. But John wrote his book without referring to any of the other books. That may be why the book of John seems so different.

If you have time, ask one student to locate the beginning of Matthew in his Bible. Ask one to find the beginning of Mark, one the beginning of Luke, and one the beginning of John. Ask each of these students to read aloud the first two or three verses to see how the different writers started their books.

2. TELLING IT LIKE IT WAS, PART 1

Before the session, photocopy for each student the Bible book names onto a sheet of adhesive-backed printer paper. When the students cut out the names, they will have small sticker labels for each book of the Bible. (Give the teacher of Discovery Center #3 enough sticker pages for the students in that group, since they are doing part 2 of this activity.) Also, find a chronological Bible (arranged in the order that the events actually happened: *The Narrated Bible*, Harvest House; *The Daily Bible*, Harvest House; *Day By Day Kid's Bible*, a children's chronological paraphrase, Tyndale).

> **MATERIALS**
> copy of Bible book names (page 77), adhesive-backed printer sheets, scissors, colored pencils, rulers, chronological Bible

DISCUSS: Ask the students if they can remember how the books of the Bible are arranged. (law, Old Testament history, poetry, prophets, New Testament history, Paul's letters, and other letters.) Say: **Because the books are in this order, they don't tell the story of Bible events in the order that they really happened. In other words, David may have written a psalm after a battle, but this psalm is not in the history section with David's story, it's in the poetry section. The prophet Joel spoke God's message during the days of King Joash, but Joel's words are not in the history section with Joash's story. Instead, Joel's book is in the prophets' section.** Display the chronological Bible and tell the students that these kinds of Bibles tell the story of the Bible in the order that the events really happened. (If this is your third group during this class time, they will have already talked about these things and you can simply review this.)

DO: Give each student a prepared sheet of the books of the Bible, scissors, colored pencils, a ruler, and his, *National Theography* folder. (Your third group will bring their sheets and folders with them.) Ask the students to fold out the Time Lines that they worked on during the last session. Then ask the students to cut out the name labels as you tell them where to stick the labels. Tell them you will go through the books in order from the regular Bible. As they place their stickers, they will be able to see that the Bible order is not the same as the order that the events really happened.

> **Genesis:** Place sticker under "Adam and Eve" and draw an arrow from there all the way across until it has underlined "Joseph becomes ruler in Egypt."
>
> **Exodus:** Place sticker under "Baby Moses is born" and draw an arrow from there until it has underlined "Ten rules and a worship tent."
>
> **Leviticus:** Place sticker under "Ten rules and a worship tent."
>
> **Numbers:** Place sticker under Leviticus.

Deuteronomy: Place sticker under Numbers.

Joshua: Place sticker under "Jericho falls."

Judges, Ruth: Place sticker under "Gideon, Samson, Ruth."

1 Samuel: Place sticker under "Saul, the First King."

2 Samuel: Place sticker under "David, the Singing King."

1 Kings: Place sticker under "Solomon, the Rich King," builds the worship house," then draw an arrow from there until the arrow has underlined "Jehoshaphat."

2 Kings: Place sticker under "Jehoram" and draw an arrow from there until the arrow has underlined "Jerusalem is torn down."

1 Chronicles: Place sticker under "Saul, the First King" and draw a line from there until it has underlined "David, the Singing King."

2 Chronicles: Place sticker under "Solomon, the Rich King, builds the worship house" and draw a line from there until it has underlined "Jerusalem is torn down."

Ezra: Place sticker under "Zerubbabel leads God's people back to Jerusalem," and draw an arrow until it underlines "Ezra leads more people back home."

Nehemiah, Esther, Job: Place sticker above their names on the time line.

Psalms: Place sticker under "Saul, the First King" and draw an arrow from there until it underlines "Solomon, the Rich King, builds the worship house." Also write Psalms under "Jerusalem is torn down" and under "The worship house in Jerusalem is built again."

Proverbs, Ecclesiastes, Song of Solomon: Place sticker under "Solomon, the Rich King, builds the worship house."

Isaiah, Jeremiah: Place sticker above their names on the time line.

Lamentations: Place sticker under "Judah taken captive by the Babylonians."

Ezekiel, Daniel, Hosea: Place sticker above their names on the time line.

DISCUSS: Remind the students that although you are reading them the books of the Bible in the order they come in the Bible, it's not the order they come on the time line. Why?

Ask the students to take their folders and sticker sheets with them to the next Discovery Center to complete this activity.

3. TELLING IT LIKE IT WAS, PART 2

If this is your first group, you will need to start the same way Discovery Center #2 starts. Otherwise, the students coming to you from group #2 will bring their sticker sheets and folders with them. Tell them that you will help them finish the activity they started in Discovery Center #2.

MATERIALS
copy of Bible book names (page 77), adhesive-backed printer sheets, scissors, colored pencils, rulers, chronological Bible

DO: Instruct the students to cut out and place their stickers as follows:

Joel, Amos, Obadiah, Jonah, Micah, Nahum, Habakkuk, Zephaniah, Haggai, Zechariah, Malachi: Place stickers above their names on the time line.

Matthew, Mark, Luke, John: Place stickers under "God's Son came" and draw an arrow from there until it underlines "Jesus' best gift."

Acts: Place sticker under "Peter and John teach, Stephen and Philip preach" and draw an arrow from there until it underlines the "Letters from Paul."

Romans, 1 & 2 Corinthians, Galatians, Ephesians, Philippians, Colossians, 1 & 2 Thessalonians, 1 & 2 Timothy, Titus, Philemon: Place stickers in the space above "Letters from Paul."

Hebrews: Place stickers under the time line after "James, Jude, and Peter write letters."

James, 1 & 2 Peter: Place stickers under "James, Jude, and Peter write letters."

1, 2, & 3 John: Place stickers under Hebrews.

Jude: Place sticker under "James, Jude, and Peter write letters."

Revelation: Place sticker under "John writes about the future."

DISCUSS: Remind the students that although you are reading them the books of the Bible in the order they come in the Bible, it's not the order they come on the time line. Why?

Discoverers' Debriefing

DISCOVERERS' DEBRIEFING

If you have time to review, gather as a large group and discuss your young discoverers' findings. Ask the following questions:

- **What is the most interesting thing you discovered today?**
- **What did you learn today that you didn't know before?**
- **Name some of the different kinds of Bibles you saw today?**
- **Do we need these different kinds of Bibles? Why or why not?**

Review the Scripture for today.

Pray, thanking God for his Word and the different forms it comes in.

Genesis	**Job**	**Habakkuk**	**1 Thessalonians**
Exodus	**Psalms**	**Zephaniah**	**2 Thessalonians**
Leviticus	**Proverbs**	**Haggai**	**1 Timothy**
Numbers	**Ecclesiastes**	**Zechariah**	**2 Timothy**
Deuteronomy	**Song of Solomon**	**Malachi**	**Titus**
Joshua	**Isaiah**	**Matthew**	**Philemon**
Judges	**Jeremiah**	**Mark**	**Hebrews**
Ruth	**Lamentations**	**Luke**	**James**
1 Samuel	**Ezekiel**	**John**	**1 Peter**
2 Samuel	**Daniel**	**Acts**	**2 Peter**
1 Kings	**Hosea**	**Romans**	**1 John**
2 Kings	**Joel**	**1 Corinthians**	**2 John**
1 Chronicles	**Amos**	**2 Corinthians**	**3 John**
2 Chronicles	**Obadiah**	**Galatians**	**Jude**
Ezra	**Jonah**	**Ephesians**	**Revelation**
Nehemiah	**Micah**	**Philippians**	
Esther	**Nahum**	**Colossians**	

The Bible in My Life

Scripture

"Your word is a lamp to my feet and a light for my path."
  Psalm 119:105

Goal

Learn that Bible study can help us grow wiser in our everyday lives.

INTRODUCTION

From magazines and newspapers, cut out ad slogans that would be appropriate for use in your classroom. For example, "We bring good things to life," or "Did somebody say McDonald's?" Place these on the walls all around your room. Set out old magazines, scissors, glue, and markers. As the students enter, give each of them a large piece of manila paper. Ask each one to look around at the slogans and then choose one that most nearly represents her and her personality. She should take that slogan from the wall and glue it to her paper. If she wants, she can cut out the company name (for example "McDonald's") and insert her own name. Then she should look through the magazines, cut out pictures that represent her interests, and glue these pictures onto the paper as well. Students can also cut out letters to spell an interest of theirs if they cannot find a picture of it (for example, soccer).

DISCOVERY RALLY

Gather the students together in a large group.

WHAT'S THE GOOD WORD?
Choose a student to read the Scripture for today.

THE CHALLENGE
Show everyone the "personality posters" the students made in the introductory activity.
Say: **God knows each of you and loves you for who you are. He will never stop loving you, no matter what.** Tell them that in their Discovery Groups today, they will learn about a way to let God teach them. (Later, you may make a gallery of these personality posters in the hallway or in your classroom.)

PRAYER

DISCOVERY CENTERS

1. TREASURE CHEST

DO: Give each student a spiral notebook and a Bible. Ask the students to design one side of the index card to make it look like a treasure chest. Then they should glue the card to the front of the notebook and write on the cover (Name)'s Treasure Chest.

> **MATERIALS**
> spiral notebooks (9 1/2" x 6"), index cards (3 1/2" x 5"), glue, tape, crayons, markers, colored pencils, a Bible for each student

DISCUSS: How do people find diamonds and rubies and other precious jewels? People have to search for these, and mine them. Tell them that the Bible is like a mine and this notebook is their treasure chest. As they read the Bible each day, it's as though they are digging in the mine to find treasures for their treasure chest, their notebook. Ask the students to take their notebooks and Bibles with them to the next Discovery Center.

If this group has already been to Discovery Center #2, ask them to copy into their journal the Scripture "treasure" which they "mined" in Discovery Center #2.

2. TREASURE HUNT

DO: Show the students a piece of paper on which you have written, in large letters, the French word *jour*. Tell the students that this is a French word that means *day*. Ask them to look carefully at the word and tell you some words in English that start with *jour*. (Journey: a day's travel, journal: the written record of what occurs daily, journalist: a person who writes daily news.) **So the treasure, or the nugget of God's Word for each day, gets written down in your daily notebook, your journal.** (Each student made, or will make, in Discovery Center #1.)

MATERIALS
paper, pencils, Bibles

If this is the first group at your center, each student will need a piece of paper and pencil. Ask the students to turn to first page of their journals, or use the paper and pencil you've given them, and write today's date at the top. Then ask the students to turn to Matthew 6. Ask them to read it silently, following along as you read it aloud. Before you read, pray aloud, asking God to give all of you wisdom and revelation as you read (Ephesians 1:17). Ask God to open your minds to understand the Scriptures (Luke 24:45). Tell the students that we are going to let God teach us now. In order to do this, any of them can call out, "Stop!" when you read
   • something that seems important for their own lives, or a friend or their family,
   • something that impresses them as being important for our nation or our world, or
   • something they never knew the Bible said, and it makes them wonder about God.

Read Matthew 6, stopping when anyone says, "Stop!" Ask the student who stopped you to copy into his journal the Scripture that caught his attention. This is a "treasure" that he or she has "mined" from the Bible today. You also may call "Stop!" once or twice to give them an example of a Scripture that has meaning for you. Explain why this Scripture seems especially important to you.

When you've finished reading, ask each student to read aloud the Scripture(s) that they copied, the things God taught them today. If some have not copied any Scriptures, ask them to choose one or two from those that other students "mined" and copy these into their journals.

Encourage students to take these journals home and use them to collect "treasures" from Scripture as they read the Bible each day. They should take their journals (the first group takes their page) and Bibles to the next Discovery Center.

3. WHAT A CHARACTER!

Before the session, make one copy of the game board for each group of 2-3 players. Also copy and cut out one set of the character cards for each group of players at your center. On the blank side of the character cards, write the character's name. Provide buttons for markers and one die for each group of players.

DO: Divide the students into groups of two or three. Give each group a game page. Give each student a button. Each student in a group should have a different color or style of button.

Explain how to play the game. All buttons start at the starting square. All cards are lined up facedown beside the game board with the character's name showing. Each student should roll the die. The one with the highest number goes first. That student rolls the die again and moves her button the number of squares indicated by the number on the die. If there is a character's name on the square, the student draws the character card and looks on back. There will be Scriptures for the student to look up and a simple question for the student to answer. The students may work together looking up the Scriptures and answering questions if they need to. Then the next person in the group does the same.

This game will give the students practice looking up Scriptures as well as applying the lessons of characters' lives to their own lives. You may need to help the students find the Scriptures, depending on the skill of the students. Tell the students that God teaches us about our lives by giving us these stories about other people and the choices they made.

Discoverers' Debriefing
DISCOVERERS' DEBRIEFING:

If you have time to review, gather as a large group and discuss your young discoverers' findings. Ask the following questions:

- **What is the most interesting thing you discovered today?**
- **What did you learn today that you didn't know before?**
- **What is a journal, and why is it helpful in Bible study?**
- **Name some ways God teaches us.**
- **How can God teach us through Bible characters' lives?**
- **What does the Bible have to do with our own lives today?**

Review the Scripture for today.

Pray, asking God to be our teacher always. Thank him for his Word and for teaching us today.

IMPORTANT: Ask students to bring photographs of themselves as babies next week (one photo per student). Their photos will be returned to them. They should bring the photos in envelopes so that no one will see the photos. You may want to send a note home with each student so parents can help their students remember.

Bible Character Cards

Joseph

Genesis 39:1-6
Genesis 39:20-23
What was he like?

Deborah

Judges 4:4
Judges 4:8-10
Judges 4:14
What did she do?

Joshua

Exodus 33:7-11
Joshua 11:15
What was he like?

Peter

John 18:7-11
John 21:4-9
What was he like?

Andrew

John 1:40-42
John 6:8
John 12:21, 22
What did he often do?

Moses

Exodus 4:8-13
Exodus 33:12, 13
Numbers 12:3
What was he like?

David

1 Samuel 30:21-25
1 Samuel 24:1-7
1 Samuel 17:17-20
What was he like?

Martha

Luke 10:40
John 12:2
**What would
she often do?**

Ruth

Ruth 1:15-17
Ruth 2:1-3
Ruth 3:1-5
What was she like?

Philip

John 1:43-46
Acts 8:5
Acts 8:26-35, 40
What did he do?

Thomas

John 14:5
John 20:24-28
What did he often do?

Mary

Luke 10:38
John 11:32
John 12:3
**Where would you
often find her?**

Guided Devotions

Scripture

"These are written that you may believe that Jesus is the Christ, the Son of God, and that by believing you may have life in his name." John 20:31

Goal

Learn what devotions are and why we need them. Learn some ways to have personal or family devotions.

NOTE: As students arrive, collect their baby photographs which you asked for last week. Use them for Discovery Center #2.

INTRODUCTION

As the students arrive, give each student a piece of copy paper on which three horizontal lines have been drawn: one 3-inches down from the top, one 6-inches down from the top, one 9-inches down from the top. Tell the students that they will help each other draw people. The head of the person will be on the top section of the paper. The body down to the waist will be in the second section down. The legs will be in the third section down, and the feet will be in the bottom section. But each student will only draw one section.

As each student is given a paper, he draws a head in the top section. Then he folds that section back so that the head cannot be seen. He gives the paper to another student. This second student draws a body on the second section, folds that section back, and gives the paper to a third student. This student draws the legs on the third section, folds that section back and gives it to a fourth student. This student draws feet on the bottom section of the page and gives the page to you. You unfold the drawing and display it by tacking it to a bulletin board or wall, or by lining up the drawings on a table. Let the students look at their portraits.

DISCOVERY RALLY

Gather the students together in a large group.

WHAT'S THE GOOD WORD?
Choose a student to read the Scripture for today.

THE CHALLENGE
Say: **Many things played a part in our growing up to become the people we are today. And many things will influence us to become the people we will be in the future.** Ask them what some of those things might be. (How we are raised, the experiences we have, the friends we have, the family members in our households, the foods we eat, our health, and so on.) **One of the most important things you can do to help yourself grow up to be a person who is loving and good, generous and kind, joyful and peaceful, is to spend time with God praying, thinking about him, listening to him, and reading his Word, the Bible. We call our time with God our devotions.** Tell the students that in their Discovery Groups today, they will learn more about devotions.

PRAYER

DISCOVERY CENTERS

1. BRAINSTORMING
Before the session, print the following letters on a piece of paper. Make the letters as large as possible. Then photocopy the paper so that each student can have a copy of it.

MATERIALS
paper, marker, colored pencils

D R E I V M O S T F I A O P N G S

DO: Give each student a prepared page of letters. Ask the students to use a pen or pencil and cross out every other letter, starting with the second letter. Then they should write the remaining letters in order across the bottom of the paper. Ask the students what the word spells (devotions).

DISCUSS: What does *devotion* mean? *Devote* means to give something totally for a specific purpose. **When we study the Bible and pray, we are taking time to celebrate God being with us, and we are giving ourselves totally to him for his purposes.**

DO: Ask the students to brainstorm. Ask the students who have family devotions at home to tell what their families do during devotions. Ask students to share any other ideas they might have about what to do during family devotions. Ask the students to write these in different colors of pencil or marker at different places on their papers.

Then ask the students to think of locations (real possibilities, not fantasy) where devotions could take place. As different locations are mentioned, ask the students to write these in different places on their paper.

Then ask the students to think of different times when devotions can be done. As these times are mentioned, ask the students to write these in different places on their papers.

If you have time, tell the students to turn the paper over now. Ask them to imagine the kind of family devotion they would most like to have. Then they should write down what they would do, in the order they would like to do it. They will have designed their own family devotion. Challenge them to take this home and encourage their family to do it sometime in the coming week. If their family can't do it, they could do it with friends, or even alone. Emphasize the importance of having time alone, one-on-one with God, even while they are young.

2. WHO'S THE BABY?

DO: Show the students's baby pictures one by one and ask your group to guess who each one is. Ask them what their favorite foods are now. Ask them if they could eat those kinds of foods when they were babies.

MATERIALS
baby pictures of students collected at the beginning of the session

DISCUSS: Just as our bodies need to mature and grow, so our spirits need to mature and grow. And just as regular foods nourish our bodies, spiritual food nourishes our spirits. What might spiritual food be? What helps our spirits grow? (Bible study, going to church and Sunday school, prayer, Scripture memory, singing and playing music to God, meditating on God and his Word.) These are things we can call devotions. These are ways of celebrating God's presence with us, and giving our lives totally to God.

3. DOING DEVOTIONS

DO: Tell students that instead of just talking about devotions, you'll do one together in this group. Sit in a circle on the floor. Ask the students to volunteer for different parts of the devotion. One student can lead an opening prayer. Some of

MATERIALS
Bibles, music tapes or CDs and tape or CD player (optional)

the students can lead songs or suggest songs they might want to sing. If you need to use a tape or CD, read some of the song titles that you have available and let the students choose two or three of them to listen to and/or sing along with. Choose a student or two to read Scriptures, and another student to say a closing prayer.

You may plan the devotion or let the students suggest the theme. Here are some different choices:
- centered around a Bible story
  (For example, the story of Naaman after Naaman is well and starts his journey home (2 Kings 5:19). Elisha's servant Gehazi lies to Naaman. Discuss the theme of honesty.)
- centered around a theme
  (For example, what does God want us to do? Why were we created? Read Jeremiah 13:11; Ephesians 2:10; Psalm 50:15; Isaiah 43:7; and Matthew 5:16. God wants us to show his greatness. He wants us to honor and glorify him. Talk about how to honor and glorify God.)

Lead the students in this devotion time.

If you have time, ask the students how a person can have devotions alone. Show them a variety of children's devotion books and periodicals such as *Family Walk* (Walk Thru the Bible, www.walkthru.org), *Sword Fighting* or *Day By Day Devotions* (Tyndale).

Discoverers' Debriefing

DISCOVERERS' DEBRIEFING:

If you have time to review, gather as a large group and discuss your young discoverers' findings. Ask the following questions:

- **What is the most interesting thing you discovered today?**
- **What did you learn that you didn't know before?**
- **What is a devotion?**
- **When and where can you have devotions?**
- **How can a person have devotions alone?**
- **Why is it important to have devotions?**

Review the Scripture for today.

Pray, thanking God for always being near us. Tell God that you devote your life to him. Ask him to guide you into having your own devotion time with him.

IMPORTANT: Remember to return the students' baby photos to them before they go home.

Making Plans

Scripture
"Man does not live on bread alone, but on every word that comes from the mouth of God." Matthew 4:4

Goal
Commit to study the Bible.
Make a plan for Bible study.

INTRODUCTION

Bring Bible times foods to celebrate the completion of this quarter of learning about God's Word. Some Bible times foods are grapes, almonds, figs, olives, pitas, raisins, honey, and bread. Enjoy snacking on these. If you want to find out about these foods in the Bible, students may look them up in their concordances and read about them. Ask students why they think God said that the promised land to which he was leading his people was "flowing with milk and honey."

Discovery Rally

DISCOVERY RALLY

Gather the students together in a large group.

WHAT'S THE GOOD WORD?

Choose a student to read the Scripture for today.

THE CHALLENGE

Ask students to briefly tell you some of the things they have learned in the past twelve weeks. Ask: **What do you think was the most fun activity you did?** Tell them that you had to make plans for each week. Ask: **What do you think might have happened if I hadn't had a plan?** What kinds of things do you and your family have to plan for? Then tell the students that studying God's Word is done best when we have a plan for doing it. In their Discovery Groups today, they will be making their own plans for studying the Bible.

PRAYER

Discovery Centers

DISCOVERY CENTERS

1. ONE-YEAR BIBLES

DO: Give each student a paper plate and markers. Say: **Many people read through the whole Bible in one year. This can be done if people read about four chapters a day. Some Bibles are made in a way that makes it easy to know how much to read each day.** Show the students how the one-year Bible is arranged. Let each student take a turn looking up his birthday and writing the proverb listed for that day in the center of the paper plate. Then each student can color and design a proverb plate, punch two holes in the top, and thread ribbon or yarn through it to hang it. Let the students take the plates home to hang in their rooms.

MATERIALS
one or more one-year Bibles that include a daily reading of an Old Testament passage, a New Testament passage, a psalm and a proverb (such as The One Year Bible, Tyndale); white paper plates, markers, hole punch, ribbon or yarn, scissors

DISCUSS: Why is it a good idea to have a plan when studying the Bible?

2. CALENDAR

DO: Along with his twelve calendar pages, give each student two pieces of colored paper to be the cover of the calendar. Ask each student to stack his pages together with one colored page on top and one colored page on the bottom. Let the students staple all layers at the top of the calendar page or punch two holes through all layers and tie the layers together with yarn. Punch a hole through all layers at the bottom of the calendar page so the calendar can be hung.

Using the calendar of the upcoming year and beginning with January, the students should write the month name on each page and number the days of each month. Then they may draw a picture to go with each month.

Tell the students that if they want to read through the Bible in a year, they will need to read about four chapters each day. And they *can* do it, if they plan for it and make a habit of it. If they miss a day, they should just keep on going, because they will eventually get through all of it if they don't give up.

If they want a plan that is not quite as overwhelming, give each student a copy of the Short Bible Reading Plan (page 96). Ask them to tape this page to the bottom of the last page of the calendar so that it hangs beneath the calendar as shown. They may trim off extra length with scissors.

MATERIALS
twelve copies of the blank calendar page (page 95) and one copy of the Short Bible Reading Plan (page 96) for each student, colored paper, stapler, paper punch, yarn, scissors, calendar for the upcoming year, colored pencils

DISCUSS: The books on this condensed list are a bit easier to read than the other books and will give the students a lot to think about. Challenge the students to plan now to read all the way through the Bible as they grow older. Ask: **Why would it be a good idea to read the whole Bible all the way through? If someone has read the Bible once, would it be necessary to read it again? Why or why not? Why do some people read the Bible over and over again? What should you do if you get behind in your Bible reading plan?**

3. WHERE AND WHEN?

DO: Give each student a piece of paper and a pen, pencil, or marker. Ask the students to think for a minute and picture in their minds the room in their house in which they plan to study the Bible. Tell them that their blank page is that room and ask them to picture on that page the drawing of that room. Then ask the following questions for them to answer by drawing.

MATERIALS
paper, pencils, markers, colored pencils

- Do you like to study with lots of light or not much light? (They can draw shades or curtains over the window in this room, or draw an open window. If it's night time in their picture, they can draw a lamp, large and bright or small.)
- Do you like the door open or closed to this room? (Draw the door opened or closed.)
- Do you like to study with music or without? (Draw a radio or tape/CD player, or leave room without one.)
- Do you like to sit at a desk, on a bed, on the floor, or somewhere else in the room? (They draw themselves in that location.)
- Do you like to eat or drink when you study? (They draw food and drink, or none.)
- What time of day do you plan to study your Bible? (Draw a clock that shows that time.)
- Do you like lots of things to look at in this room? (Draw pictures on the wall, posters, and so on.)
- Do you like this room organized or a bit messy? (Draw it.)

Let the students complete the drawings of this room if they wish.

DISCUSS: Tell students that different people like to study in different ways. There is no wrong way or right way. **What's important is that you have a plan for studying your Bible, and that once you start, you make it a habit.**

DISCOVERERS' DEBRIEFING:

If you have time to review, gather as a large group and discuss your young discoverers' findings. Give each student a Bible. The following Bible versions may be helpful:

- *International students's Bible*
- *New International Reader's Version*
- *New Living Translation*
- *Contemporary English Version*

Readability is an important issue when encouraging children to read and study God's Word on their own. Even though Bibles may have a younger reading level, readability is not just a matter of using simpler words. Larger type size and a comfortable spacing between the lines help as well. Some Bibles may be readable at the word level, but be difficult for children to read because of the tiny type and narrow spacing.

If you want your students to get an overview of the Scriptures, every book placed in the order in which the events actually happened, the abridged paraphrased Bible *Day By Day Kid's Bible* (Tyndale House Publishers) is a good choice (2nd grade reading level).

Ask the following questions:
- **What is the most interesting thing you discovered today?**
- **What did you learn today that you didn't know before?**
- **Why is it important to have a plan for reading the Bible?**
- **Why does God want us to read and study his Word?**
- **Why is God's Word called the sword of the Spirit?**
- **What do you do if you get behind in your Bible study plan?**

Review the Scripture for today.

Pray, thanking God for his Word and asking God to help each student to establish a habit of reading and studying his Word. Ask God to make his Word come alive in their hearts and to guide each student closer to him as they study their Bibles.

IMPORTANT: Make sure that the students take home their *National Theographic* folders as well as their new Bibles and any other paperwork or artwork they have made this quarter.

Sunday	Monday	Tuesday	Wednesday	Thursday	Friday	Saturday

Short Bible Reading Plan

JANUARY Genesis: 1-50 (2 chapters a day for 25 days)	**FEBRUARY** Exodus 1-28 (1 chapter a day)	**MARCH** Exodus 29-40 Judges 1-19 (1 chapter a day)
APRIL Judges 20, 21 1 Samuel 1-18 (1 chapter a day)	**MAY** 1 Samuel 29-31 2 Samuel 1-24 Ruth 1-4 (1 chapter a day)	**JUNE** Psalm 1-150 (5 chapters a day, except for Psalm 119; read it in one day)
JULY Proverbs 1-31 (1 chapter a day)	**AUGUST** 1 Kings 1-22 2 Kings 1-9 (1 chapter a day)	**SEPTEMBER** 2 Kings 10-25 Jonah 1-4 Esther 1-10 (1 chapter a day)
OCTOBER Daniel 1-6 Matthew 1-25 (1 chapter a day)	**NOVEMBER** Matthew 26-28 John 1-21 Acts 1-6 (1 chapter a day)	**DECEMBER** Acts 7-28 James 1-5 (1 chapter a day)

Made in the USA
Middletown, DE
19 March 2019